CONGREGATION FC
OF CONSECRATED LIFE
AND SOCIETIES OF APOSTOLIC LIFE

PROCLAIM

TO CONSECRATED MEN AND WOMEN
WITNESSES OF THE GOSPEL AMONG PEOPLES

All documents are published thanks to the generous support of the members of the Catholic Truth Society

CATHOLIC TRUTH SOCIETY
PUBLISHERS TO THE HOLY SEE

CONTENTS

First published 2016 by The Incorporated Catholic Truth Society 40-46 Harleyford Road London SE11 5AY Tel: 020 7640 0042 Fax: 020 7640 0046. Translated by Christina Cooley.

ISBN 978 1 78469 162 2

“The Church was born catholic, that is,
‘symphonic’ from her very origins
projected to evangelisation
and encounter with all,
she was born ‘outward-bound’,
that is, missionary”.

(Pope Francis)

Dear brothers and sisters,

1. The echo of the celebration of the Year of Consecrated Life resounds in our hearts with Pope Francis's call addressed to us: wake up the world, follow the Lord in a prophetic way, be heralds of the joy of the Gospel. In his exhortations, we are reminded of St John Paul II's affirmation: "The Church needs the spiritual and apostolic contribution of a renewed and revitalised consecrated life".[1]

This Dicastery has received a lot of positive feedback on experiences that consecrated men and women from every continent had in Rome during this Holy Year of grace for the Church: the prayer vigils that opened all of the convocations and the eucharistic celebrations that closed them, the ecumenical meeting of consecrated people of different Churches, the meeting for formators, the meeting for consecrated youth, the special time that called all forms of consecrated life into communion. The Holy Father Francis accompanied each event with a familiar and fraternal dialogue, indicating the broad horizons and prophetic nature of a life lived in the form of the Gospel in the Church.

We give thanks to God, who is "Goodness, all Goodness, the greatest Goodness",[2] for this event of the Spirit. Our gratitude goes out to those who passionately worked on planning and making this special time possible and to those who answered the convocation to the See of Peter to be part of the event in a sign of unity. We give special thanks to Pope Francis for having given us this Year and for having accompanied us during this time as the Successor of Peter and as one who, like us, is consecrated to God.[3]

2. Today, we continue our journey of reflection embarked upon together through the Letters *Rejoice*, *Keep Watch* and *Contemplate*. Our journey stops to read the *missio Dei* as the mystery entrusted by Christ to his Church and confirmed at Pentecost with the power of the Holy Spirit: *You will receive power when the Holy Spirit comes on you, and then you will be my witnesses not only in Jerusalem but throughout Judaea and Samaria,*

---

[1] John Paul II, Post-Synodal Apostolic Exhortation *Vita Consecrata* (25th March, 1996), 13.

[2] Saint Francis, *The Praises of God*, in FF 261.

[3] Cf. Francis, Apostolic Letter *To all Consecrated People on the Occasion of the Year of Consecrated Life* (21st November, 2014).

and indeed to the ends of the earth (*Ac* 1:8). Every form of consecrated life receives, accepts and lives this call as the constitutive element of the special *sequela Christi*. Fifty years after its promulgation (28th October, 1965), the final exhortation of the *Perfectae Caritatis* resounds with rich vividness: "Let all religious, therefore, rooted in faith and filled with love for God and neighbour, love of the cross and the hope of future glory, spread the Good News of Christ throughout the whole world so that their witness may be seen by all and our Father in heaven may be glorified (cf. *Mt* 5:16)".[4] Pope Francis accompanies us in this revisitation with the inspiring and performative language that he uses consistently, both for the universal Church and for our form of life. Let's continue this dialogue that from the other Letters with all consecrated men and women so that our intellect, heart and decisions may foster life and so the insights of the Year of Consecrated Life may bear fruit.

To all of you, consecrated men and women, we express our gratitude for your dedication to God, the ray of divine beauty that enlightens the path of human existence.[5] We also invite you to continue writing your story in the tongue of fire in the power of the Holy Spirit. The tongue you will use to proclaim the Good News will have words, assonances, accents, nuances and facts that differ from your way of living the consecration. Whether in the totally contemplative life or in the apostolic religious life, in the praise of the virgin heart, in the presence, hard work and witness within local churches, or in the secularity of social environments, may you always be an expression of the Church's mission. Fragrance of the Holy Spirit and joy of the Gospel in the human city.

May Mary, "whose life is a model for all",[6] accompany our journey and intercede, *Mater misericordiae*, for a joyous prophetic devotion to the Gospel.

---

[4] Vatican II Ecumenical Council, Decree on the Adaptation and Renewal of Religious Life *Perfectae Caritatis* (28th October, 1965), 25.

[5] Cf. John Paul II, Post-Synodal Apostolic Exhortation *Vita Consecrata* (25th March, 1996), 109.

[6] Saint Ambrose, *De Virginitate*, l. II, c. II, n. 15.

PROLOGUE

"Evaluate the times and change with them,
remaining steadfast in the truth of the Gospel".

(Pope Francis)

WE INHABIT THE WORLD

3. Our time is characterised by a profound and continuous process of change whose features we struggle to define.

Visions of life that, placed on the same level, relativise the value of each are increasing: the person, family, friendship, love, work, commitment and death are all considered differently. Ethnocultural plurality is growing; people pass quickly through a variety of experiences and the availability of endless possibilities, causing fragmentation and dispersion. People live life as if they are in a large supermarket filled not only with things, but with opportunities, ideas, and behaviours that all create the risk and the challenge of choosing, of defining oneself, of finding personal reasons for one's own behaviours. The sense of limit that accustoms people to avoiding the obstacles that normally define and outline desires and actions is changing. Individualism, the emphasis on the self and personal needs, makes interpersonal relationships more fragile, and it considers every bond to be changeable, never definitive, even in the most important choices, such as a person's state of life.

It is a cultural process that is alive and ongoing in which modernity, with the principle of universality being crushed, sees itself as liquid post-modernity. The sense of dissatisfaction and uncertainty that come with this pace and a consumeristic and competitive way of life - where one must fend off others to take centre stage - sentences us to living in the permanent uncertainty that is the cause and effect of emotional precariousness and the instability of relationships and values. The "liquid" characters of life and society nourish and strengthen each other, since neither of them is able to keep its own shape or maintain the route towards a desired and established destination for very long.

4. We consecrated men and women are often surrounded and daunted by this process. Overwhelmed by the complexity of the times, we forget our attitude of listening to the human cry as well as the spiritual significance of proclaiming the Gospel which, even in difficult contexts, can reawaken "the assent of the heart by its nearness, love and witness".[1]

---

[1] FRANCIS, Apostolic Exhortation *Evangelii Gaudium* (24th November, 2013), 42.

We must not stop asking ourselves questions about the today of God and about the opportunities and problems presented to the Church's mission by the times we live in and by the changes that characterise them. We are called to labour and to the joy of listening in the culture of our time so that we may discern the seeds of the Word, the "traces of God's presence":[2] listening to the hopes and dreams of our contemporaries, taking their desires and quests seriously, trying to understand what inflames their heart and what, on the other hand, causes them fear and mistrust or plain indifference, so we can become collaborators in their joy and hope (cf. *1 Co* 1:24).

5. We must question ourselves about "what it is that God and people today are asking".[3] Men and women suffer from the loss of identity; they are immersed in numerous identities, often virtual, that serve as masks and change according to the occasion.

During a general audience in 1969, Pope Paul VI let the words of the *autores* resound: "Tell me, Euthydemus, have you ever been to Delphi? Yes, certainly; twice. Then did you notice somewhere on the temple the inscription 'Know thyself'? I did. And did you pay no heed to the inscription, or did you attend to it and try to consider who you were? Indeed I did not; because I felt sure that I knew that already". Is is from here that "the story of the great problem regarding man's awareness of himself" begins, the Pope continues. "The activism of today and the prevalence of sensitive knowledge and social communications about speculative study and inner work makes us tributaries of the outside world and greatly diminishes personal reflection and knowledge of the questions that are inherent to our subjective lives. We are distracted, empty of ourselves and full of images and thoughts that do not necessarily regard us intimately".[4]

6. Even the attitude towards religious experience and the transcendent dimension of life has changed. Uncertainty about solitude being the definitive word on human destiny brings men to give in to the temptation of a "spiritual desertification" which leads to the "spreading of the void".[5]

---

[2] John Paul II, Post-Synodal Apostolic Exhortation *Vita Consecrata* (25th March, 1996), 79.

[3] Francis, Apostolic Letter *To all Consecrated People on the Occasion of the Year of Consecrated Life* (21st November, 2014), II, 5.

[4] Paul VI, *General Audience* (12th February, 1969).

[5] Cf. Benedict XVI, *Homily* for the Opening of the Year of Faith (11th October, 2012).

At times, we find ourselves in front of the complete theoretical and practical denial of the possibility of the Christian experience and the denial of the value and dignity of the person. What used to be Christian identity was lost long ago in the phenomenon that Weber defines as the "disenchantment of the world". Western culture frees itself from a sacred vision and celebrates the autonomy of man and society. Reality presents itself as complexity.

A vision emerges that is not only anthropologic and naturalistic, but historical, social, cultural and religious; a vision in which the individual, in his plural dimensions and numerous possibilities, recognises himself to be insecure and uncertain in his actions, but at the same time, capable of journeys, recoveries, openness. In this context, the religious issue emerges as a matter of sense (meaning and direction), freedom and happiness to be read into and interpreted.

7. Against disenchantment, which presents a world deprived of all meaning and all possibility of consolation, arises the re-enchantment of the world as a different vision and provocative interpretation of reality, but above all, of man's inner universe and his deep feeling: "The reaction against an abstract, quantified, objectified universe is realised through a return to the wellsprings of affectivity".[6]

Against the denial of the kingdom of the invisible, a faint return to the marvelous appears. We catch a glimpse of new scenarios, even though they can seem of the ephemeral. Reading and criticising them, interpreting their requests, could become space for the spirit in which to recognise the soul.

In this context, we must consider the interlocutor of the Gospel proclamation and his life in the today of history: "The great suffering of man is this: behind the silence of the universe, behind the clouds, is or isn't there a God? And, if this God is there, does he know us, does he have anything to do with us? Is this God good, and does the reality of good have any power in the world or not? Is he a reality or not? Why do we not hear him?"[7]

---

[6] E. MORIN *Lo Spirito del Tempo*, Meltemi Editore, Rome 2005, 93.

[7] BENEDICT XVI, *Meditation* during the First General Congregation of the XIII Ordinary General Assembly of the Synod of Bishops (8th October, 2012).

8. Our time calls us to create projects of meaning in which the culture of a new Christian humanism can generate - in the inconsistent fluidity and ungovernable complexity of technological progress - the ability to give meaning to existence and a horizon of communication, understanding and values to live by. The light of the Good News can re-enchant the world with the possibility of reigniting a journey towards the truth: "A renewal of preaching", Pope Francis writes in *Evangelii Gaudium*, the document he defined as the outline for his own Petrine ministry, "can offer believers, as well as the lukewarm and the non-practising, new joy in the faith and fruitfulness in the work of evangelisation. The heart of its message will always be the same: the God who revealed his immense love in the crucified and risen Christ. God constantly renews his faithful ones, whatever their age: *They shall mount up with wings like eagles, they shall run and not be weary, they shall walk and not be faint* (*Is* 40:31). Christ *is the eternal Gospel* (*Rv* 14:6); he is the same yesterday and today and forever (*Heb* 13:8), yet his riches and beauty are inexhaustible. He is for ever young and a constant source of newness".[8]

9. Consecrated persons are called to show this eternal beauty to the world: "The first duty of the consecrated life is to *make visible* the marvels wrought by God in the frail humanity of those who are called. They bear witness to these marvels not so much in words as by the eloquent language of a transfigured life, capable of amazing the world",[9] "the new evangelisation demands that consecrated persons have a thorough awareness of the theological significance of the challenges of our time".[10]

We are called to inhabit human contexts with depth and radicality so we can give a face and an expression to the traces of God's presence.[11] This presence is not a superfluity of man; it is his depth, his truth. It is about never distancing ourselves from our own self truth or from relationships with others and with creation. It is about experiencing the 'sequela' of Christ as a way of making room, thanks to him, for human truth.

---

[8] FRANCIS, Apostolic Exhortation *Evangelii Gaudium* (24th November, 2013), 11.

[9] JOHN PAUL II, Post-Synodal Apostolic Exhortation *Vita Consecrata* (25th March, 1996), 20.

[10] *Ibid.*, 81.

[11] Cf. *Ibid.*, 79.

Blessed Paul VI observes: "The conditions of the society in which we live oblige all of us therefore to revise methods, to seek by every means to study how we can bring the Christian message to modern man. For it is only in the Christian message that modern man can find the answer to his questions and the energy for his commitment of human solidarity".[12]

At the conclusion of the ordinary session of the thirteenth General Synod of Bishops[13] dedicated to the new evangelisation for the transmission of the faith, Benedict XVI called for new ardour and new methods: "The Church seeks to adopt new methods, developing new language attuned to the different world cultures, proposing the truth of Christ with an attitude of dialogue and friendship rooted in God who is Love. In various parts of the world, the Church has already set out on this path of pastoral creativity, so as to bring back those who have drifted away or are seeking the meaning of life, happiness and, ultimately, God".[14]

---

[12] PAUL VI, *Address* to the Sacred College of Cardinals (22nd June, 1973).

[13] 17-28th October, 2012.

[14] BENEDICT XVI, *Homily* on the Occasion of the Holy Mass for the Closing of the XIII Ordinary General Assembly of the Synod of Bishops (28th October, 2012).

TO THE ENDS OF THE EARTH

You will be my witnesses not only in Jerusalem
but throughout Judea and Samaria,
and indeed to the ends of the earth.
(*Ac* 1:8)

LISTENING

10. "The image of Christ the Teacher was stamped on the spirit of the Twelve and of the first disciples, and the command: *Go...and make disciples of all nations* set the course for the whole of their lives. St John bears witness to this in his Gospel when he reports the words of Jesus: *No longer do I call you servants, for the servant does not know what his master is doing; but I have called you friends, for all that I have heard from my Father I have made known to you*. [...] For this reason he formally conferred on them after the resurrection the mission of making disciples of all nations".[1] *Go out to the whole world; proclaim the Good News to all creation* (*Mk* 16:15). *You will be my witnesses not only in Jerusalem but throughout Judea and Samaria, and indeed to the ends of the earth* (*Ac* 1:8). This is the missionary mandate that the Risen Christ leaves his disciples. It is a mandate for every disciple, in every age. This mandate has a universal dimension; disciples are sent to all the nations (*Mt* 28:19), *to the whole world* (*Mk* 16:15), *to all the nations* (*Lk* 24:47). The Lord assures the disciples that they will never be alone: *I am with you always; yes, to the end of time* (*Mt* 28:20). The Gospel of Mark attests: *While they, going out, preached everywhere, the Lord working with them and confirming the word by the signs that accompanied it* (*Mk* 16:20).

11. Each of the evangelists presents mission with a specific emphasis, and together they complete each other. The differing ways of the evangelists show how mission is called to respond to the community's various situations, and at the same time, they reveal the imagination of the Spirit who blows where it pleases (cf. *Jn* 3:8), dispensing its charisms. Mark presents mission as proclamation or *kerygma* (cf. *Mk* 16:15). In Matthew, the purpose of mission is the foundation of the Church and on teaching (cf. *Mt* 28:19-20, 16:18). Luke presents mission as witness (cf. *Lk* 24:48; *Ac* 1:8). For John, mission consists in sharing in the communion between the Father and the Son (cf. *Jn* 17:21-23). There is only one objective: confessing with Peter: *You are the Christ* (*Mk* 8:29), or with the Roman centurion: *Truly this man was a son of God* (*Mk* 15:39).[2]

---

[1] JOHN PAUL II, Apostolic Exhortation *Catechesi Tradendae* (16th October, 1979), 10.

[2] Cf. JOHN PAUL II, Encyclical Letter *Redemptoris Missio* (7th December, 1990), 23.

The *Acts of the Apostles* show us how the disciples will progressively focus in on their identities as witnesses and proclaimers and how they will find the right lexicon and style needed to live out their missionary mandate in different situations and cultures. The disciples found themselves facing new contexts and challenges. They allowed themselves to be led by the *Spirit of truth* (*Jn* 16:13) down unknown paths so they could preserve with love and proclaim with joy all that the Master had said and taught (cf. *Mt* 28:20; *Jn* 14:26). This same Spirit, Jesus had assured them, would have lead them to *the complete truth*, opening the journey of the Gospel to *the things to come* (*Jn* 16:13), in other words, to new existential and salvific answers in the days ahead.

12. The missionary mandate is also defined in various ways: proclaiming the Good News to all the nations (cf. *Mt* 28:19; *Mk* 16:15); bearing witnesses to the resurrection (cf. *Lk* 24:46-48; *Ac* 1:8); being bearers of peace and reconciliation (cf. *Jn* 20:21-23); caring for the sick and helping the excluded (cf. *Lk* 10:1-9); being the light of the world and salt of the earth (cf. *Mt* 5:13-16); loving one another as Jesus himself had loved (cf. *Jn* 13:34-35) and serving and washing the feet of our brothers (cf. *Jn* 13:12-15). The disciples quickly understood that they were to follow the mission that Jesus had announced in the synagogue of Nazareth when he proclaimed the words of the prophet Isaiah: *The spirit of the Lord has been given to me, for he has anointed me. He has sent me to bring the Good News to the poor, to proclaim liberty to captives and to the blind new sight, to set the downtrodden free, to proclaim the Lord's year of favour* (*Lk* 4:18-19).

An immense cultural and geographical horizon opens up before the small group of disciples who are still amazed by what they experienced during the final weeks of the Master's life and who are uncertain about the future; only with time will they come to know, evangelise and inhabit this new horizon. Only the gift of the Spirit will help them understand the profound meaning of those words and will make them capable of fulfilling a task which, humanly speaking, was beyond their abilities and which seemed paradoxical.

13. Mission, as an extension of the Master's mission, is the foundation of our vocation as consecrated men and women. Our Founders and Foundresses heard, recognised and accepted Jesus's imperative as if it were addressed directly to them: *Go and proclaim!* (cf. *Mk* 16:15). Consecrated life, in all of its forms and various seasons and in different contexts, has embarked on a journey to "fill all the earth with Christ's Gospel",[3] placing itself on the vanguard of mission and persevering with fervent, creative and *heartfelt devotion* (cf. *Ac* 11:23).

Let us assume the Gospel as rule and life,[4] *sent by the Holy Spirit* (*Ac* 13:4) towards every periphery where the light of the Gospel is needed (cf. *Mt* 5:13-16); let us assume the world with our hearts turned to the Lord, and let us proclaim with our life and word the *Good News of Jesus Christ, Son of God* (*Mk* 1:1) that is the sign of hope for all, especially for the poor (cf. *Lk* 4:18). This is how we will restore the joy of the Gospel that we have received by grace.[5]

SENT TO PROCLAIM

14. "The Church's fundamental function in every age and particularly in ours is to direct man's gaze, to point the awareness and experience of the whole of humanity towards the mystery of Christ".[6]

Jesus lives on the shore of the lake in Capernaum and is in contact with many people: he attends the synagogue, meets the crowd, heals the sick. Jesus goes where the people live.[7] In his message, in his actions and in his choices, he expresses a dynamism that moves in the direction of universal openness.

---

[3] THOMAS OF CELANO, *The First Life of Saint Francis*, 97, in FF 488.

[4] Cf. BENEDICT XVI, Post-Synodal Apostolic Exhortation *Verbum Domini* (30th September, 2010), 83.

[5] Cf. FRANCIS, Apostolic Exhortation *Evangelii Gaudium* (24th November, 2013), 1.

[6] JOHN PAUL II, Encyclical Letter *Redemptor Hominis* (4th March, 1979), 10.

[7] Cf. A. VANHOYE, *Le Origini della Missione Apostolica nel Nuovo Testamento*, in *La Civiltà Cattolica*, 141 (1990/IV), 544-558.

IN CHRIST'S WAY

15. Let us contemplate Christ, missionary of the Father,[8] to proclaim in his way: *Jesus made a tour through all the towns and villages, teaching in their synagogues, proclaiming the Good News of the kingdom and curing all kinds of diseases and sickness. And when he saw the crowds he felt sorry for them!* (*Mt* 9:35-36). We must enter into the dynamic of seeing, of being moved to compassion and acting - attitudes that characterised the life and mission of Christ. Seeing means paying attention to what happens in the world and being open to the reality that surrounds us, not only out of mere curiosity, but in order to recognise God's appearance in history.

Being moved to compassion means living with *depths of mercy*; it requires participation and action for those who are on the edge and who are in need: *So as he stepped ashore he saw a large crowd; and he took pity on them* (*Mk* 6:34). A powerful movement takes place which puts us in friendly accord with each person: *While he was still a long way off, his father saw him and was moved with pity. He ran to the boy, clasped him in his arms and kissed him tenderly* (*Lk* 15:20). This attitude does not allow us to pass by absently, self-righteously or fearfully: *Now a priest happened to be travelling down the same road, but when he saw the man, he passed by on the other side. In the same way a Levite who came to place saw him, and passed by* (*Lk* 10:31-32). We are reminded of Christ's judgement of our choices and deeds: *For I was hungry and you never gave me food* [...] *I tell you solemnly, in so far as you neglected to do this to one of the least of these, you neglected to do it to me* (*Mt* 25:42,45)

We are called to experience the quiver of those who dissent deep down because of wounded and unfair justice and an arrogant violence that kills, abuses, cancels and marginalises: "The Church", Paul VI affirms, "cut to the quick by this cry, asks each and every man to hear his brother's plea and answer it lovingly".[9]

16. We are called to act according to God's vision: *I have seen the miserable state of my people in Egypt. I have heard their appeal to be free of their slave-drivers. Yes, I am well aware of their sufferings*

[8] Cf. John Paul II, Post-Synodal Apostolic Exhortation *Vita Consecrata* (25th March, 1996), 22.

[9] Paul VI, Encyclical Letter *Populorum Progressio* (26th March, 1967), 3.

(*Ex* 3:7). We are called to attune our hearts Christ's way, *at the sight of her tears, and those of the Jews who followed her, Jesus said in great distress, with a sigh that came straight from the heart, "Where have you put him?" They said, "Lord, come and see". Jesus wept* (*Jn* 11:33-35). We are called to carry out actions that ignite hope and tell the story of salvation. Without acting, seeing and being moved to compassion remain good intentions and vague emotions.

The Apostolic Letter *Orientale Lumen* by John Paul II said it well: "We learn from the Lord himself, who would stop along the way to be with the people, who listened to them and was moved to pity when he saw them *like sheep without a shepherd* (*Mt* 9:36; cf. *Mk* 6:34). From him we must learn the loving gaze with which he reconciled men with the Father and with themselves, communicating to them that power which alone is able to heal the whole person".[10]

CONTEMPLATIVES IN ACTION

17. Missionary mystique must be salvaged: "It is from contemplation, from a strong friendship with the Lord that the capacity is born in us to live and to bring the love of God, his mercy, his tenderness, to others".[11] Apostolic mystique refers us to "what is most beautiful, most grand, most appealing and at the same time most necessary".[12]

We invite you to reread the Letter *Contemplate* in which we proposed an itinerary towards the depth of the mystery that lives in us, on the quest for Beauty; a new *Philokalia*: the transfiguration created by hospitable sanctity and empathetic nearness.[13]

"The missionary must be a 'contemplative in action'. He finds answers to problems in the light of God's word and in personal and community prayer. [...] the future of mission depends to a great extent on contemplation. Unless the missionary is a contemplative he cannot proclaim Christ in a credible way. He is a witness to the experience of

---

[10] JOHN PAUL II, Apostolic Letter *Orientale Lumen* (2nd May, 1995), 4.

[11] FRANCIS, *Angelus* (21st July, 2013).

[12] FRANCIS, Apostolic Exhortation *Evangelii Gaudium* (24th November, 2013), 35.

[13] Cf. CONGREGATION FOR INSTITUTES OF CONSECRATED LIFE AND SOCIETIES OF APOSTOLIC LIFE, *Contemplate. To Consecrated Men and Women on the Trail of Beauty* (15th October, 2015), LEV, Vatican City 2015.

God, and must be able to say with the apostles: *That which we have looked upon, concerning the word of life* [...] *we proclaim also to you* (*1 Jn* 1:1-3)".[14]

18. "The Church cannot illude herself into thinking that she shines with her own light. Saint Ambrose expresses this nicely by presenting the moon as a metaphor for the Church: 'The moon is in fact the Church: [...]' she shines not with her own light, but with the light of Christ. [...] To the extent that the Church remains anchored in him, to the extent that she lets herself be illumined by him, she is able to bring light into the lives of individuals and peoples. For this reason the Fathers of the Church saw in her the *mysterium lunae*. We need this light from on high if we are to respond in a way worthy of the vocation we have received. To proclaim the Gospel of Christ is not simply one option among many, nor is it a profession. For the Church, to be missionary does not mean to proselytise: for the Church to be missionary means to give expression to her very nature, which is to receive God's light and then to reflect it".[15] Without this awareness, our work and institutions cannot communicate the Good News of the Kingdom; our formative programs become itineraries of professional qualification which are more or less successful; the concerns we have about our economic means that we feel are limited to sustaining the life and work of our Institutes do not differ from those of other human groups; we often forget the parameters of providence.

SERVANTS OF THE WORD

19. Scripture, together with Tradition, is the "supreme rule"[16] of faith. Scripture and evangelisation in its many forms are closely related: "The Church's deepest nature is expressed in her three-fold responsibility: of proclaiming the word of God (*kerygma-martyria*), celebrating the sacraments (*leitourgia*), and exercising the ministry of charity (*diakonia*). These duties presuppose each other and are inseparable".[17]

---

[14] JOHN PAUL II, Encyclical Letter *Redemptoris Missio* (7th December, 1990), 91.

[15] FRANCIS, *Homily* for the Epiphany of the Lord (6th January, 2016).

[16] VATICAN II ECUMENICAL COUNCIL, Dogmatic Constitution *Dei Verbum* (18th November, 1965), 21.

[17] BENEDICT XVI, Encyclical Letter *Deus Caritas Est* (25th December, 2005), 25a.

Go and proclaim (cf. *Mk* 16:15). "At the beginning of this new millennium, the Church's mission is to be nourished by the Word through being a servant of the Word in the work of evangelisation".[18] A Word that is *alive and active* that *can judge the secret emotions and thoughts* (*Heb* 4:12) and that is "'ever more fully at the heart of every ecclesial activity'. [...] It is essential that the revealed word radically enrich our catechesis and all our efforts to pass on the faith".[19]

Pastoral experience shows that we cannot presume to find faith in those who listen to us. Faith must be rekindled in those whose faith has been extinguished, it must be reinvigorated in those who live in indifference, with personal effort it must be revealed to new generations, it must be renovated in those who profess it without sufficient conviction, it must be taken to those who do not know it yet.

20. Catechesis, the first educational act of the mission of evangelisation, "is intimately bound up with the whole of the Church's life. Not only her geographical extension and numerical increase, but even more, her inner growth and correspondence with God's plan depend essentially on catechesis".[20]

In *Evangelii Gaudium*, Pope Francis invites us to take a mother's tone, a mother's way of speaking.[21] "Just as all of us like to be spoken to in our mother tongue, so too in the faith we like to be spoken to in our 'mother culture', our native language (cf. *2 M* 7:21, 27), and our heart is better disposed to listen. This language is a kind of music which inspires encouragement, strength and enthusiasm".[22] We are called to serve the Word, starting with the concreteness of our lives and with real words that are full of maternal tenderness and that know how to question and enliven reality. It is fundamental to meditate on the Word, to understand it in depth and to translate in into words suitable for the culture of each age, even through careful study.

---

[18] SYNOD OF BISHOPS, XII Ordinary General Assembly *The Word of God in the Life and Mission of the Church, Instrumentum Laboris* (Vatican City 2008), 43.

[19] FRANCIS, Apostolic Exhortation *Evangelii Gaudium* (24th November, 2013), 174-175.

[20] JOHN PAUL II, Apostolic Exhortation *Catechesi Tradendae* (16th October, 1979), 13.

[21] Cf. FRANCIS, Apostolic Exhortation *Evangelii Gaudium* (24th November, 2013), 139-141.

[22] *Ibid.*, 139.

21. Presumption and superficiality present in the various forms of proclamation - homiletic, catechetical, pastoral - are an offense to the gift of the Word. Pope Francis insisted on homilies and the effort they require: "Preparation for preaching is so important a task that a prolonged time of study, prayer, reflection and pastoral creativity should be devoted to it".[23] Studying, done as a way to serve the Word and humanity, helps us interpret the world that *God loved so much* (*Jn* 3:16) and to understand it with wisdom. Studying that does not "extinguish the spirit of prayer"[24] is more than an academic and rhetorical exercise, is an exercise in the meditation required to advance in the enthusiasm of the quest for the Life, the Truth and the Good (cf. *Ac* 17:27). Studying, the "expression of the unquenchable desire for an ever deeper knowledge of God, the source of light and all human truth", must accompany our lives as a valuable tool in "the constant quest for the presence and activity of God in the complex reality of today's world".[25]

ONES WHO BRING GOOD NEWS

22. *How beautiful on the mountains, are the feet of one who brings good news, who heralds peace, brings happiness, proclaims salvation, and tells Zion, "Your God is king!"* (*Is* 52:7)

"The characteristic of every authentic missionary life is the inner joy that comes from faith. In a world tormented and oppressed by so many problems, a world tempted to pessimism, the one who proclaims the *Good News* must be a person who has found true hope in Christ".[26]

Proclamation is passion given by grace and placed at the centre of our life. "To the question, 'why mission?' we reply with the Church's faith and experience that true liberation consists in opening oneself to the love of Christ. In him, and only in him, are we set free from all alienation and doubt, from slavery to the power of sin and death. Christ is truly *our peace* (*Ep* 2:14); *the love of Christ impels us* (*2 Co* 5:14), giving meaning and joy to our life. Mission is an issue of faith, an accurate indicator of our faith in Christ and his love for us".[27]

---

[23] *Ibid.*, 145.

[24] SAINT FRANCIS, *Letter to Saint Anthony of Padua*, 2.

[25] JOHN PAUL II, Post-Synodal Apostolic Exhortation *Vita Consecrata* (25th March, 1996), 98.

[26] JOHN PAUL II, Encyclical Letter *Redemptoris Missio* (7th December, 1990), 91.

[27] *Ibid.*, 11.

Pope Francis invites us to not be 'dejected and discouraged evangelisers who look like someone who has just come back from a funeral',[28] but to convey the joy of faith, starting with a transfigured existence.[29]

23. *Messengers of the joy of the Gospel* are men and women who have received the mandate to proclaim the Good News; the joy of the Gospel has filled their lives and transformed their hearts.[30]

Messengers of the joy of the Gospel are men and women who respond with generosity to the great challenge of the Church of all ages: missionary activity.[31]

Messengers of the joy of the Gospel are men and women touched by the Father's mercy, a wound of love that inflames their hearts with the passion for Christ and humanity, and who offer their lives for the Gospel and begin a journey that instant (cf. *Lk* 24:33) to proclaim the joy of the Kingdom "to all, in all places, on all occasions".[32]

Messengers of the joy of the Gospel are men and women who take initiative,[33] not allowing themselves to be paralysed by ecclesial introversion,[34] to reach the peripheries of society in order to meet people *near and far* (cf. *Ep* 2:13), excluding no one.

Messengers of the joy of the Gospel are men and women who stand at the crossroads of life and experience the frontiers, welcome outcasts[35] so that their lives may be filled with the hope and liberating power of the Gospel.

Messengers of the joy of the Gospel are men and women who "go forth"[36] and reach the whole world (cf. *Mt* 28:19) to proclaim with creativity and the universal language of joy that the Gospel is the source of life and life in full (cf. *Jn* 10:10b).

---

[28] Francis, Apostolic Exhortation *Evangelii Gaudium* (24th November, 2013), 10.

[29] Cf. John Paul II, Post-Synodal Apostolic Exhortation *Vita Consecrata* (25th March, 1996), 35.

[30] Cf. Francis, Apostolic Exhortation *Evangelii Gaudium* (24th November, 2013), 21.

[31] Cf. *Ibid.*, 15.

[32] *Ibid.*, 23.

[33] Cf. *Ibid.*, 24.

[34] Cf. *Ibid.*, 27.

[35] Cf. *Ibid.*, 24.

[36] *Ibid.*, 20.

The Church and the world need men and women who are heralds (*mevasser*), messengers of joy, messengers of he who comes to console his people (cf. *Is* 40:1).

UNITED TO PROCLAIM

24. *The whole group of believers was united, heart and soul; no one claimed for his own use anything that he had, as everything they owned was held in common. The apostles continued to testify to the resurrection of the Lord Jesus with great power, and they were all given great respect* (*Ac* 4:32-33). "The religious community has felt itself to be in continuity with the group of those who followed Jesus. He had called them personally, one by one, to live in communion with himself and with the other disciples, to share his life and his destiny (cf. *Mk* 3:13-15), and in this way to be a sign of the life and communion begun by him".[37] Fraternal life, mindful of the mystery that exists at its origin, is experienced as "God-enlightened space in which to experience the hidden presence of the Risen Lord".[38]

PERSEVERING IN COMMUNION

25. The *Didache* outlines the features of community identity as the work of listening and formation and the knowledge of the person and of the mission of the Lord Jesus, accompanied by signs and power (cf. *Ac* 2:43, 4:33). Christians of the early Church listen to the preaching and the message of the apostles and so, are introduced to the knowledge of the Gospel, bringing mature believers to a true experience with the Lord.

One of the concerns felt throughout the history and life of the Church as well as in the existence of various communities of consecrated life, is about forming to the mystery of Christ that enlivens *koinōnía*, the essence of fraternal life, and that manifests it not as an idea, but rather as material and spiritual solidarity.

[37] CONGREGATION FOR INSTITUTES OF CONSECRATED LIFE AND SOCIETIES OF APOSTOLIC LIFE, *Fraternal Life in Community "Congregavit nos in unum Christi amor"* (2nd February, 1994), 10.

[38] JOHN PAUL II, Post-Synodal Apostolic Exhortation *Vita Consecrata* (25th March, 1996), 42.

26. Fraternity demands perseverance in *the breaking of the bread and in the prayers* (*Ac* 2:42), a golden sign aimed at identifying the cultish meetings of early Christians where Jesus's gestures from the last supper are relived. This also includes the wedding feasts, Jesus's banquets with sinners, and the frugal meals consumed by the Risen Christ on the shore of the lake with his disciples. Early Christians pray in temples, during meals or in the privacy of their own homes with different forms of prayer. The persevering relationship with God is at the base of the spiritual teaching of the primitive community which prayed constantly, on every possible occasion (*Ep* 6:18), in every place and lifting their hands up reverently (*1 Tm* 2:8). Prayer ensures community unity and helps discernment; it is a gift from the Spirit and is so closely connected to charity that Origen says, "He 'prays without ceasing' who unites prayer to works and good works to prayer. Only in this way can we consider as realisable the principle of praying without ceasing".[39] We are at the heart of the missionary witness of fraternity.

27. An air of joy and of new origins reaches us and wins over the hearts of all who participate in this rebuilding of a new humanity. It is an air that has always enchanted Christians of all generations and people who are consecrated to the 'sequela' of Christ. "The life of that [first] community and, even more, the experience of complete sharing with Christ lived out by the Twelve, have always been the model to which the Church has looked whenever she has sought to return to her original fervour and to resume with fresh evangelical vigour her journey through history".[40]

Missionary witness and proclamation in the sign of communion come from this air: none of their members was ever in want (*Ac* 4:34) because the community was united, heart and soul (*Ac* 4:32). Every apostolic community that wants to be evangelical holds the detachment from material goods in their heart. It is an indispensable prerequisite for finding accord of spirits, for reaching the goals of spiritual life and for proclaiming the Good News.

---

[39] ORIGEN, *De Oratione* 12, in *PG* 11, 452c.

[40] JOHN PAUL II, Post-Synodal Apostolic Exhortation *Vita Consecrata* (25th March, 1996), 41.

28. *The apostles continued to testify to the resurrection of the Lord Jesus with great power* (*Ac* 4:33). Luke affirms that the grace of witnessing the Risen Christ arises from fraternal life, the parable of the Kingdom, and in itself as missionary proclamation. The joy of proclaiming the Good News is strengthened by the experience of fraternal encounter. Pope Francis invites: "Living the present with passion means becoming 'experts in communion', 'witnesses and architects of the plan for unity which is the crowning point of human history in God's design'. In a polarised society, where different cultures experience difficulty in living alongside one another, where the powerless encounter oppression, where inequality abounds, we are called to offer a concrete model of community which, by acknowledging the dignity of each person and sharing our respective gifts, makes it possible to live as brothers and sisters".[41]

The life of communion becomes a *sign* for all the world and a compelling *force* that leads people to faith in Christ. In this way communion leads to *mission*, and itself becomes mission.[42]

29. In religious life, fraternal life in community, lived in simplicity and joy, is the primary and fundamental structure of evangelisation. "Fraternal communion, as such, is already an apostolate; in other words, it contributes directly to the work of evangelisation. The sign par excellence left us by our Lord is that of lived fraternity: *by this all will know that you are my disciples, if you have love for one another* (*Jn* 13:35). [...] The effectiveness of religious life depends on the quality of the fraternal life in common. Fraternal life is not the *entirety* of the mission of a religious community, but it is an essential element. Fraternal life is just as important as apostolic life".[43]

---

[41] Francis, Apostolic Letter *To all Consecrated People on the Occasion of the Year of Consecrated Life* (21st November, 2014), I, 2.

[42] Cf. John Paul II, Post-Synodal Apostolic Exhortation *Vita Consecrata* (25th March, 1996), 46.

[43] Congregation for Institutes of Consecrated Life and Societies of Apostolic Life, *Fraternal Life in Community "Congregavit nos in unum Christi amor"* (2nd February, 1994), 55.

IN THE PRODIGY OF THE PENTECOST

30. The first Pentecost, with the explosion of the Spirit and the enthusiasm of the first mass conversion, ends in an unexpected way. Many people begin to live a fraternal lifestyle. The Spirit pours forth and the unattainable dream of fraternity is made possible: to feel like brothers and sisters and to live in fraternity. Of all the miracles, prodigies and signs, this is the most shocking: people who do not know each other understand each other and, by putting their personal goods together, speak the same language of charity. Something that was believed to be impossible is ignited in the world: the love for others becomes stronger than the love for oneself. Fraternity, the prodigy of the Pentecost, shows the Church's true nature and becomes the main reason for the spreading of the Good News. Freemen and slaves, rich men and poor men, intellectual men and ignorant men, are all brought together around the same table to live out the prophecy of God's children in Christ, in the power of the Spirit.

31. The experience of the Spirit and of fraternity lived in community are at the origins of the Church. The Holy Spirit acts in the life of the apostolic community and distinguishes it, in the seal of fire, with unity and missionarity. God's Word, the language of the Spirit, descends upon man and leads the community of faith to use the human language, the means of comprehension of the other person, rather than imposing his language to proclaim the Good News. "Whenever we encounter another person in love, we learn something new about God. […] The work of evangelisation enriches the mind and the heart; it opens up spiritual horizons; it makes us more and more sensitive to the workings of the Holy Spirit, and it takes us beyond our limited spiritual constructs".[44]

[44] Francis, Apostolic Exhortation *Evangelii Gaudium* (24th November, 2013), 272.

32. This is the work of the Spirit which opposes the *flesh* (cf. *Ga* 5:16-17), that is, the self-indulgence of man, the introversion, the rejection of encounter and communion with others. "The movement of love between heaven and earth is guided by the Holy Spirit, and in this way he completes the relationship, established in Christ, with Zion, Mary and *Ekklesia* as Bride. The religious person lives in the middle of this event that wants to become reality even in him and for him through his loving devotion to love. His existence must always be creative translation, future of God permanently in the Holy Spirit".[45]

[45] H. U. VON BALTHASAR, *Spiritus Creator* Morcelliana, Brescia 1972, 328.

CHURCH WHICH "GOES FORTH"

As they visited one town after another,
they passed on the decisions reached
by the apostles and elders in Jerusalem,
with instructions to respect them.
So the churches grew strong in the faith,
as well as growing daily in numbers.

(*Ac* 16:4-5)

33. Paul is the protagonist, along with Silas and Timothy and possibly other companions who are not mentioned. The apostle is experiencing a difficult change; he has just separated from Barnabas, his protector and master, after a rather *violent quarrel* (*Ac* 15:39). But he does not stop; he returns to visit the communities they founded together on the first missionary journey (cf. *Ac* 13:5; 14:28).

We choose this key moment in the early Church because, in the choices and difficulties of Paul and his friends, we find situations very similar to our own and a quest for solutions that can guide us in facing the complexity of problems and uncertainties that we experience as well.

The communities founded on the previous trip were Derbe, Lystra, Pisidian Antioch, Iconic and Attalia, that is, the mountainous central region of present-day Turkey on the Anatolian plateau. Paul had planned on moving north with his friends towards Galatia and Bithynia, but more than once the Spirit mysteriously hindered their itinerary and their good intentions. They find themselves forced to head in the direction of Troas (cf. *Ac* 16:6-8), towards unknown lands.

All of the communities they visited were in the beginning stages of their faith and were fragile. They had been entrusted to elders on the first missionary journey and were aware that they would have to *experience many hardships before entering the kingdom of God* (*Ac* 14:22b). It was logical and wise for Paul and his friends to go back and visit these communities so they could encourage them on their journeys and perfect the first evangelisation, increasing attendance as well. Yet, for no apparent reason, *the Spirit of Jesus would not allow them to.* Surprise and concern lead them to roam, moving further and further towards Western Anatolia until they arrive at the coast of the Aegean Sea.

We can only imagine their inner distress, their sense of frustration and the feeling of finding themselves facing the unknown.

34. In many ways, this adventure resembles situations from recent decades. The reform and renewal that was promoted and prompted by the Second Vatican Council made room for meaningful experiences and created, for almost all religious families, new ways of presence and encounters with

previously unknown cultures and places. As with Barnabas and Paul after the first missionary journey, with the joy of seeing that the Lord called people who did not know each other to participate in charism and his ecclesial fecundity, there were many times when tensions ran high, arguments were heated and souls were overheated (cf. *Ac* 15:2).

While the differences in cultures and identities of the Churches of new members were initially embraced with enthusiasm and wonder, over time, they caused unease and posed problems regarding differences to respect, essentiality to rediscover, right and necessary reciprocity within the whole of the institutional system, and models of incarnation of faith. With hard work and patience it was decided - through the Chapters and Assemblies, the redaction or revision of Constitutions and the experimentation with models of formation and governance - to write out a summary supporting communion through institutional forms suitable to the new period of charism. We were convinced that all we had to do to keep the journey moving forward was to inform adequately and manage intelligently the decision that had already been reached through much effort and decided upon methodically, as Paul had done when he *transmitted* the decisions made in Jerusalem (cf. *Ac* 16:4).

35. Just like with Paul and his friends, the Spirit *would not allow* (cf. *Ac* 16:7) us to enter into the attitude of custody and maintenance of results. He kept us from branching out according to our plans by simply exporting preordained decisions and tried models.

Couldn't the current crisis, which is making our certainties useless and our plans uncertain, have something to do with the frustration that Paul felt in the face of inexplicable obstacles? Could our stubbornness to persevere with what we have established and stabilised, with mere strategic arrangements and often by concealing the crisis of orientation as "spiritual worldliness", perhaps be considered a *kairòs* to leave room for the unpredictability of the Spirit and his indications?

Could the evident and widespread insignificance and marginality of consecrated life in the Church and in a globalised society that is narcotised by thousands of idolatries and ephemeral illusions, our *anaemia* of fresh forces and the clear *anaemia* of successful models for this new context be compared to Paul's confusion and disorientation at *Troas*? There where nothing seemed to make sense, a new horizon and a new creative and transformative adventure will open up.

36. God, who is Trinitarian Love, is the first missionary: the Church's mission is rooted in the heart of God. There is a continuous movement between the three persons of the Trinity, a "dance" as Saint Bonaventure would say.[1] In the relationship between the Father and the Son, the grace of love that is the Holy Spirit is given: *ad extra*, the Son is sent by the Father for the Spirit and the Spirit is sent by the Father and by the Son and by the Father for the Son. In the Word made man (cf. *Jn* 1:14), it is God himself who "goes forth"[2] and enters into the world and takes on human form: "For he sent his Son, the eternal Word, who enlightens all men, so that he might dwell among men and tell them of the innermost being of God (cf. *Jn* 1:1-18)".[3] Incarnation reveals to us a God who loves humanity: "Jesus Christ, therefore, the Word made flesh, was sent as 'a man to men'. He 'speaks the words of God' (*Jn* 3:34), and completes the work of salvation which his Father gave him to do (cf. *Jn* 5:36, 17:4)".[4] Nothing is unknown to him, not even sin, which is removed by his mercy.[5] *For our sake God made the sinless one into sin, so that in him we might become the goodness of God* (2 *Co* 5:21).

The God of history walked with his people (cf. *Ex* 3:6) and does not cease to walk with us through the gift of the Spirit. "It is the Holy Spirit who gives life":[6] He is the power of God in history, he who points out and actualises the Word (cf. *Jn* 14:26; *1 Jn* 2:27).[7] The Holy Spirit, principal agent of mission,[8] "is the principal agent of evangelisation: it is he who impels each individual to proclaim the Gospel, and it is he who in the depths of consciences causes the word of salvation [...] He alone stirs up

---

[1] Saint Bonaventure, *Itinerarium Mentis in Deo*, VI, 2: this text uses the word *circumincessio*.

[2] Cf. Francis, Apostolic Exhortation *Evangelii Gaudium* (24th November, 2013), 20.

[3] Cf. Vatican II Ecumenical Council, Dogmatic Constitution on Divine Revelation *Dei Verbum* (18th November, 1965), 4.

[4] *Idem*.

[5] Cf. Francis, Spiritual Retreat on the Occasion of the Jubilee for Priests, *First Meditation* (2nd June, 2016).

[6] John Paul II, Encyclical Letter *Dominum et Vivificantem* (18th May, 1986), 64.

[7] Cf. *Ibid*., 7.

[8] Cf. John Paul II, Encyclical Letter *Redemptoris Missio* (7th December, 1990), 21.

the new creation, the new humanity of which evangelisation is to be the result, with that unity in variety which evangelisation wishes to achieve within the Christian community. Through the Holy Spirit the Gospel penetrates to the heart of the world, for it is he who causes people to discern the signs of the times - signs willed by God - which evangelisation reveals and puts to use within history".[9]

37. The Spirit forms Christians according to the mind of Christ, guides to all the truth, enlightens, puts love in our hearts, strengthens weak bodies, opens us up to the awareness of the Father and of the Son and gives "joy and ease to everyone in assenting to the truth and believing it".[10]

During the ecumenical meeting in Uppsala in 1968, the Orthodox Metropolitan Ignatius di Latakia had this to say: "Without the Holy Spirit, God is far away, Christ stays in the past, the Gospel is a dead letter, the Church is simply an organisation, authority, a matter of domination, mission, a matter of propaganda, the liturgy, no more than an evocation, Christian living, a slave morality. But in the Holy Spirit, the cosmos is resurrected and groans with the birth pangs of the Kingdom; the risen Christ is there; the Gospel is the power of life; the Church shows forth life of the Trinity; authority is a liberating service; mission is a Pentecost; the liturgy is both memorial and anticipation; human action is deified".[11]

Like it did with Paul, the power of the Spirit *does not allow* (cf. *Ac* 16:7) us to stop moving forward and our logic to limit and rationalise our missionary decisions to what we already know. When hopes dwindle, the breath of the Spirit leads us towards new horizons. "We must overcome the temptation to restrict ourselves to what we already have, or think we have, safely in our possession: it would be sure death in terms of the Church's presence in the world; the Church, for that matter, *can only be missionary, in the outward movement of the Spirit*".[12]

---

[9] PAUL VI, Apostolic Exhortation *Evangelii Nuntiandi* (8th December, 1975), 75.

[10] VATICAN II ECUMENICAL COUNCIL, Dogmatic Constitution on Divine Revelation *Dei Verbum* (18th November, 1965), 5.

[11] IGNATIUS DI LATAKIA, in R. CANTALAMESSA, *Il Soffio dello Spirito*, San Paolo, Cinisello Balsamo 1997, 165.

[12] BENEDICT XVI, *Homily* on the Occasion of the Apostolic Journey to Portugal on the 10th Anniversary of the Beatification of Jacinta and Francisco, Young Shepherds of Fátima, Porto (14th May, 2010).

VOCATION AND GRACE OF THE CHURCH

38. The Church's mission is a project born of the love of God the Father, or *amor fontalis* as it is called by the Fathers of the Church, who wanted us to participate, through the Son and the Spirit, in his divine life.[13] Thanks to the deliberation of the Second Vatican Council, the Church recovered the Trinitarian concept of mission, recognising herself as a collaborator. Benedict XVI affirmed, "we should learn the simplest and most fundamental lesson of the Council: namely, that Christianity in its essence consists of faith in God which is Trinitarian Love".[14] The Church finds its identity in mission. Paul VI wrote, "Evangelising is in fact the grace and vocation proper to the Church, her deepest identity. She exists in order to evangelise, that is to say, in order to preach and teach, to be the channel of the gift of grace".[15]

In *Evangelii Gaudium*, Pope Francis calls upon all People of God to live "permanently in a state of mission".[16] He comes to identify the very life of the Church with mission; "My mission of being in the heart of the people is not just a part of my life or a badge I can take off; it is not an 'extra' or just another moment in life.

Instead, it is something I cannot uproot from my being without destroying my very self. I am a mission on this earth; that is the reason why I am here in this world. We have to regard ourselves as sealed, even branded, by this mission of bringing light, blessing, enlivening, raising up, healing and freeing".[17] The missionary mandate of Jesus is a resonance of the communion of Trinitarian love and an invitation to give it, under the impulse of the Spirit, a concrete expression in time and space. The Church only has meaning as a means of communicating this love. She participates in God's mission in this way.

---

[13] Cf. VATICAN II ECUMENICAL COUNCIL, Decree on the Mission Activity of the Church *Ad Gentes* (7th December, 1965), 1-4.

[14] BENEDICT XVI, *General Audience* (10th October, 2012).

[15] PAUL VI, Apostolic Exhortation *Evangelii Nuntiandi* (8th December, 1975), 14.

[16] FRANCIS, Apostolic Exhortation *Evangelii Gaudium* (24th November, 2013), 25.

[17] *Ibid*., 273.

39. "God himself can create his Church, that God is the first agent: if God does not act, our things are only ours and are insufficient; only God can testify that it is he who speaks and has spoken. Pentecost is the condition of the birth of the Church [...] God is always the beginning".[18]

In *Evangelii Gaudium*, Pope Francis reminds us, "though it is true that this mission demands great generosity on our part, it would be wrong to see it as a heroic individual undertaking, for it is first and foremost the Lord's work, surpassing anything which we can see and understand. Jesus is 'the first and greatest evangeliser'. In every activity of evangelisation, the primacy always belongs to God, who has called us to co-operate with him and who leads us on by the power of his Spirit".[19]

The Spirit decides Paul's steps and the destination of his journey. The apostle is perplexed and uncertain about a journey that seems to move forward without developing what has already been sown.

40. We are used to thinking that we have been sent to spread something that belongs to us, that has been entrusted to only us. Our task is to watch out for, to sense, to recognise in human places the seed that sprouts and grows. It is up to us to take care of it, freeing the field of everything that hinders growth so that the seeds can bear abundant crop (cf. *Mt* 13:4-9, 19-24). This is humility of missionary service. "The real newness is the newness which God himself mysteriously brings about and inspires, provokes, guides and accompanies in a thousand ways. The life of the Church should always reveal clearly that God takes the initiative, that *he has loved us first* (*1 Jn* 4:19) and that *he alone gives the growth* (*1 Co* 3:7)".[20]

In fact, mission is not proselytism or practical activism, it is communication of love in the power of the Holy Spirit. "Let us therefore preserve our fervour of spirit. Let us preserve the delightful and comforting joy of evangelising [...] May it mean for us - as it did for John the Baptist, for Peter and Paul, for the other apostles and for a multitude of splendid evangelisers all through the Church's history - an interior enthusiasm that

[18] BENEDICT XVI, *Meditation* during the First Congregation of the XIII Ordinary General Assembly of the Synod of Bishops (8th October, 2012).

[19] FRANCIS, Apostolic Exhortation *Evangelii Gaudium* (24th November, 2013), 12.

[20] *Idem*.

nobody and nothing can quench. May it be the great joy of our consecrated lives. And may the world of our time, which is searching, sometimes with anguish, sometimes with hope, be enabled to receive the Good News not from evangelisers who are dejected, discouraged, impatient or anxious, but from ministers of the Gospel whose lives glow with fervour, who have first received the joy of Christ, and who are willing to risk their lives so that the kingdom may be proclaimed and the Church established in the midst of the world".[21]

WITNESSES IN THE CHURCH

41. Mission is more than diakonia and apostolic works; it covers all dimensions of our life of special consecration that is called to "become mission",[22] to become the proclamation of the Good News of the Kingdom of God and the recognition and prophecy of its silent presence among us. Consecrated men and women "at the deepest level of their being are caught up in the dynamism of the Church's life, which is thirsty for the divine Absolute and called to holiness. It is to this holiness that they bear witness. They embody the Church in her desire to give herself completely to the radical demands of the beatitudes. By their lives they are a sign of total availability to God, the Church and the brethren. As such they have a special importance in the context of the witness which, as we have said, is of prime importance in evangelisation".[23]

We participate in the Church's mission in full, overcoming the limits of our Institutes. Every form of consecrated life is therefore called to make what the Church endorses and indicates as her mission in the modern world visible in its life and good works.

The invitation resounds as an urgent imperative: recognise where the Spirit is directing us through the demands that the Church makes of us and think of ways to listen and encounter so as to harmonise the charisms and projects of communion with evangelical courage. All consecrated life in its many forms - virginal, monastic, apostolic, secular - is missionary.

---

[21] Paul VI, Apostolic Exhortation *Evangelii Nuntiandi* (8th December, 1975), 80.

[22] Cf. John Paul II, Post-Synodal Apostolic Exhortation *Vita Consecrata* (25th March, 1996), 72.

[23] Paul VI, Apostolic Exhortation *Evangelii Nuntiandi* (8th December, 1975), 69.

THE ORIGINS: AN INVITATION TO THE GOSPEL

42. In his Apostolic Letter addressed to all consecrated persons, Pope Francis invites us to gratitude, passion and hope.[24] The Church's gratitude towards consecrated persons whose "apostolate is often marked by an originality, by a brilliance that demands admiration. They are generous: often they are found at the outposts of the mission, and they take the greatest of risks for their health and their very lives. Truly the Church owes them much".[25] The missionary history of consecrated men and women lived out in religious Family, Order, Congregation and Institute honours and fecundates the Church over the centuries. Our history shines with witness of sanctity and stories of martyrs that told and tell of the primacy of God, the creativity of the Spirit and its transformative power in the lives of people, fraternities and active collectives marked by the Gospel. From the cloister of contemplative Orders - where lives of peoples has always resounded - to the pulpits of knowledge, to rural schools and provinces, from parish communities to places where illnesses are cured, from the chapels where we pray to the streets of the world where we proclaim, to community centres, to the forges where work makes time sacred, and from dispensaries to shelters, to the crossroads of the forgotten and the homeless, consecrated life has tried to be a sign of God's nearness.

Our Founders and Foundresses, obedient to the action of the Spirit, accepted his charisms so that his Church could shine in the world. Pope Francis affirms, "the most beautiful experience, though, is the discovery of all the different charisms and all the gifts of his Spirit that the Father showers on his Church! [...] And when the Church, in the variety of her charisms, is expressed in communion, she cannot be mistaken: it is the beauty and the power of the *sensus fidei*, of that supernatural sense of faith which is bestowed by the Holy Spirit".[26]

43. Within the variety of wounded human situations, the Spirit gave rise to diakonia, initiative and brilliance through his charisms that offered the ointment of solidarity and tenderness, dignity and hope. In their origins

---

[24] Francis, Apostolic Letter *To all Consecrated People on the Occasion of the Year of Consecrated Life* (21st November, 2014).

[25] Paul VI, Apostolic Exhortation *Evangelii Nuntiandi* (8th December, 1975), 69.

[26] Francis, *General Audience* (1st October, 2014).

and throughout their many stages of development, all of our Families have known the blossoming of unexpected mediations and of new journeys of fraternity and prophetic diakonia.

Let us not forget the grace of the origins, the humility and the smallness of beginnings that made God's work transparent in the lives and messages of those who were full of wonder and who set out on their journeys along unpaved roads and unbeaten paths. For us, the origins of our history in the Church will always be an invitation to the purity of the Good News, a blazing horizon full of the Holy Spirit's creativity, an agon by which we can measure our truth as disciples and missionaries.

The Pentecost of our origins may be far off; the sound of *a powerful wind* may fall silent, the *tongues of fire* (cf. *Ac* 2:1-3) may not be visible to our eyes of the flesh and it could seem as though we are mute. Like Paul, we would like to go back to the lands and among the people we already know. We are tempted by what is already done, by the quest for daily certainties, for known journeys and for visibility that is far from the Gospel's way. "I invite you to have a faith that can recognise the wisdom of weakness. In the joys and afflictions of the present time, when the harshness and weight of the cross make themselves felt, do not doubt that the *kenosis* of Christ is already a paschal victory. Precisely in our limitations and weaknesses as human beings we are called to live conformation with Christ in an all-encompassing commitment which anticipates the eschatological perfection, to the extent that this is possible in time. In a society of efficiency and success, your life, marked by the 'humility' and frailty of the lowly, of empathy with those who have no voice, becomes an evangelical sign of contradiction".[27]

44. Consecrated life, attentive to the signs of the times and places, has known how to respond with creativity, courage and real "genius",[28] as Blessed Paul VI wrote in *Evangelii Nuntiandi*, to the spiritual, cultural and social needs that arose, while always passing through the paschal mystery of the Lord. Participating in the joys and pains of humanity has shown the most human aspect of the Church.

---

[27] Benedict XVI, *Homily* for the Feast of the Presentation of the Lord, 17th Day 'Mondiale' of Consecrated Life (2nd February, 2013).

[28] Cf. Paul VI, Apostolic Exhortation *Evangelii Nuntiandi* (8th December, 1975), 69.

We have been present in places of pain, ignorance, exclusion and lack of meaning, places where the horizon would darken until finally going out in the night.

We have been beside those who seek the face of God in daily life and sometimes in the tiring flow of human affairs, and in solidarity, we have shared our bread and our time, our joy and our hope.

More than a few people have found hospitality and company within religious communities and their works that have given them the motivation and strength to start living again.

45. The Church's missionary history coincides in large part with the history of consecrated life. Over the course of the centuries, many consecrated persons have crossed the frontiers of their home countries for the work of the Spirit, like when Paul and his friends set sail towards Troas (cf. *Ac* 16:6-8). Many of them knew how to show deep appreciation for people they met and their cultures. In the past, they helped defend them from the threats of colonisers; today, they defend cultures to protect them from those who control the processes of globalisation out of disdain for the cultural singularity of minorities. In every age, consecrated men and women have contributed to the dialogue between cultures and religious traditions, fostering dignity and identity for many peoples who had been marginalised and humiliated by the powers of the time.

The various expressions of mission (initiatives, works, options, presences, deeds) born of the charisms of Orders, Congregations, Societies of Apostolic Life and Secular Institutes make up the Church's remarkable and bright patrimony that has contributed to keeping its missionary energy alive.

AWARE OF WEAKNESS

46. Today we are asked to welcome grace and limits with the courage of discernment. We are called to conversion. We have inherited many institutions and projects from the past that have been instruments at the service of the Church and society. The Lord's call has not always found its desired echo in the hearts of consecrated persons and their institutions. Our history has not always been written in the language of transparency and love required by Gospel proclamation, the mission entrusted by Jesus to his

Church. There have been times when the lack of evangelical witness has debased the message's credibility. At times, there has been evangelisation with imposition and with a sense of superiority, abusing human liberty. Missionaries have not always known how to recognise the presence of God in the cultures and traditions they found in the places they were sent.

Our judgement, according to the Gospel, often had to regret our inability to be close to those who wanted to share their desperation and hope with us. We acknowledge with regret that there have been situations in which our people and our Communities - Orders, Institutes, Societies - have let themselves be pulled into the orbit of the powerful and rich in order to share their ideas and style, betraying the commitment to the poor and the excluded. At times, the temptation of worldliness, present in many, often subtle, forms, has gained victory over our evangelical choices. Fear has blocked our freedom to denounce that which is opposed to God's plans.

It humiliates us to think how often the missionary task has been damaged by the monopolistic and short-sighted self-centredness of one's works, by the reciprocal distrust in the shared responsibility and by the idolatry of one's founders. It has anguished us in recent decades to have betrayed the trust of families who entrusted us with their children and youth for formative courses.

We listen with humility to the voices of people and of events that, from the peripheries, continue to require our loyalty. The memory of our origins can help us to regain trust in the power of the Spirit. I have neither silver nor gold, but I will give you what I have: in the name of Jesus Christ the Nazarene, walk! (*Ac* 3:6).

"WE CANNOT LEAVE THINGS AS THEY ARE"

47. The heart of Christian proclamation is inescapably social, and the Holy Spirit that "seeks to penetrate every human situation and all social bonds" [29] knows how to "untangle the knots of even the most complex and impenetrable human affairs".[30] Therefore, "an authentic faith - which is never comfortable or completely personal - always involves a deep desire

---

[29] FRANCIS, Apostolic Exhortation *Evangelii Gaudium* (24th November, 2013), 178.

[30] JOHN PAUL II, *General Audience* (24th April, 1991).

to change the world, to transmit values, to leave this earth somehow better that we found it".[31] We must move forward following two guidelines, both of which are necessary and urgent.

The first is the renewal of ordinary pastoral ministry, which should be aimed at seizing every opportunity to let the freshness of the Good News be known. The second is made up of new missionary proposals and initiatives to be put into action with creativity and courage. In both cases, we are called to show the beauty of Christ in a credible way. If it is true that the Church "has never tired of making known to the whole world the beauty of the Gospel",[32] it is no less true that, in the face of the crisis of modern totality and the triumph of post-modern fragmentation, it is now more urgent than ever to propose to the people of our time that *whole in the fragment*,[33] the beauty that saves.

PRINCIPLES OF *EVANGELII GAUDIUM*

48. In his Exhortation *Evangelii Gaudium*, Pope Francis offers four key principles to guide us in "building a people in peace, justice and fraternity"[34] and to help us put into practice what we have heard and learned from the Word and from the poor. These guidelines, the Pope underlines, "also apply to evangelisation" and are valid "within each nation and in the entire world".[35] They are guiding principles, standards that everyone can aspire to, in politics and economics, in society and in the Church. Especially in her mission to proclaim the Good News.

In stating these four principles, the Holy Father starts with a vision of the Church as a polyhedron that is the union of all its parts and that, in its unity, maintains the distinctiveness of all the individual parts.[36]

---

[31] FRANCIS, Apostolic Exhortation *Evangelii Gaudium* (24th November, 2013), 183.

[32] BENEDICT XVI, Apostolic Letter in the form of *Motu Proprio Ubicumque et Semper* (21st September, 2010).

[33] H. U. VON BALTHASAR, *Il Tutto nel Frammento*, Jaca Book, Milano 1972.

[34] FRANCIS, Apostolic Exhortation *Evangelii Gaudium* (24th November, 2013), 221.

[35] *Idem*.

[36] Cf. *Ibid*., 236.

49. *Time is greater than space.*[37] Time begins the processes that require knowing how to wait; we need to initiate processes rather than occupy spaces of power. We must patiently favour the beginning of processes regardless of the quest for immediate results and the control that our sense of responsibility and our good intentions could lead us to. The encyclical *Lumen Fidei* points out that "space hardens processes, whereas time propels towards the future and encourages us to go forward in hope".[38] The parable of the wheat and darnel (cf. *Mt* 13:24-30, 36-43) provides an evangelical example.

"Reaching a level of maturity where individuals can make truly free and responsible decisions calls for much time and patience. As Blessed Peter Faber used to say: 'Time is God's messenger'".[39]

50. *Unity prevails over conflict.*[40] We are called to accept conflicts and to bear their weight without washing our hands of them, but also without becoming trapped by them, so that we can transform them into new processes that allow for communion in differences and that are received as such. "Communion also consists in confronting together and in a united fashion the most pressing questions of our day, such as life, the family, peace, the fight against poverty in all its forms, religious freedom and education. In particular, New Movements and Communities are called to co-ordinate their efforts in caring for those wounded by a globalised mentality which places consumption at the centre, neglecting God and those values which are essential for life".[41]

51. *Realities are more important than ideas.*[42] In his third principle, Pope Francis reaffirms the prevalence of reality with strength and effectiveness. This idea - as previously mentioned - is the result of a thought process that always runs the risk of falling victim to sophistry and so, detaching from

---

[37] Cf. *Ibid.*, 222-225.

[38] FRANCIS, Encyclical Letter *Lumen Fidei* (29th June, 2013), 57.

[39] FRANCIS, Apostolic Exhortation *Evangelii Gaudium* (24th November, 2013), 171.

[40] Cf. *Ibid.*, 226-230.

[41] FRANCIS, *Address* to Participants in the Third World Congress of Ecclesial Movements and New Communities (22nd November, 2014).

[42] Cf. FRANCIS, Apostolic Exhortation *Evangelii Gaudium* (24th November, 2013), 231-233.

reality. For the Pope, realities are always superior to ideas. Within our Institutes, we risk formulating logical and clear proposals, document after document, that deviate from our reality and the reality of the people we are sent to. We let ourselves become caught up in the newness of projects and initiatives and we forget that the most important change depends on us and our desire and ability to make it happen.

The logic of incarnation (*1 Jn* 4:2) is the guideline of this principle. "Not to put the word into practice, not to make it reality, is to build on sand, to remain in the realm of pure ideas and to end up in a lifeless and unfruitful self-centredness and gnosticism".[43] This is even more valuable in our digital society that is inundated with words, information, facts, images and intellectual chatter that often reduces faith, politics and personal and social relationships to mere rhetoric.

52. *The whole is greater than the part.*[44] We are called expand our vision so as to always recognise the greater good. This principle should be understood according to the image of the polyhedron that composes differences. These differences must be supported by a culture of dialogue as a laborious quest for the general interest: we are invited to find ties and relationships to articulate that which is non-homogeneous on different levels (from more local to more global) and in different environments (from more material to more spiritual).

RAISING QUESTIONS

53. Charisms in consecrated life, primarily founding charisms, must shine with this ecclesial paradigm. Presently, it seems as though consecrated life has lowered the missionary anchor in ports that are tried, safe, private. This is how sailing is abandoned on Peter's boat: although risky, and at times, in the middle of the billows, it always has the security of Jesus Christ's presence (cf. *Mk* 4:35-41). Effort and the grace of discernment are needed so that founding charisms pose questions about the emergencies in history that require a response. Identifying problems, questions and responses is the decisive starting point for every form of consecrated

---

[43] *Ibid.*, 233.

[44] Cf. *Ibid.*, 235-237.

life. Our missionary responses cannot be based solely on the criterion of efficacy and efficiency. Instead, they should be based on the evaluation of the credibility and evangelical reliability of the gift of the Spirit entrusted to us for the good of the Church. "Are our ministries, our works and our presence consonant with what the Spirit asked of our Founders and Foundresses? Are they suitable for carrying out today, in society and the Church, those same ministries and works? Do we have the same passion for our people, are we close to them to the point of sharing in their joys and sorrows, thus truly understanding their needs and helping to respond to them?".[45]

Our mission is space of creativity produced by the encounter of charism with history. A charism that excludes itself from ecclesial comparison and from history, thereby limiting itself to a closed circuit, risks transforming communities into a space for only initiates of alleged strong identity. In reality, it sentences itself to a weak identity focused on itself, without horizon. We invite you to look at your own charismatic and missionary experience with truth so that it is not just a name that identifies the Institute, but the relationship that was born between the Founders, the times that followed them, and history, creating the history of salvation. The present does allow closed horizons. The mission must be re-evaluated, not only within the horizon of *communio Ecclesiarum*, an ecclesiological given of no return, but especially, in the awareness that today other horizons invade and segment ours.

A PEDAGOGY OF RELIABILITY

54. Charismatic identity becomes mission when it transforms into a personal, collective and ecclesial project. We are invited to raise and pose questions without the demand for immediate answers, which leave us with the restlessness to question ourselves again. It is the root of a mission that projects beyond our horizon. When individuals and fraternities practically remove the desire and the tension to pose questions to themselves, they experience a phenomenon of domesticated resignation where routine becomes quiet life and diversities lose importance.

[45] FRANCIS, Apostolic Letter *To all Consecrated People on the Occasion of the Year of Consecrated Life* (21st November, 2014), I, 2.

Motivation and demotivation. In the Western world an inevitable reduction in numbers and a new demand for apostolic reliability are taking place. The first, in many cases, has slowed down the regeneration of resources: lack of new vocations, decrease in numbers, increase in deaths, casting off of property and cessation of apostolic work. The second, while less perceived, is a process of progressive demotivation of the individual consecrated persons or fraternities and communities that generates indifference towards any kind of change. Motivation is the resource *par excellence* that allows us to identify possible ecclesial synergies for shared service, even when resources are scarce. Motivation combined with the realistic assessment of resources clarifies the chance of supporting orientations of change and requires functional decisions. Being able to evaluate expectations of the future - avoiding alarmism - helps prepare possible strategies.

Diffusive process. Planning is ideation, that is, a diffusive process: ideas are transmitted by contagion. An attitude of open-mindedness, and especially of conversion, is needed: let us rework our common patrimony of norms, values and mental maps to revive it.

Without accepted and shared motivations, it is unlikely that individuals, communities and Institutes will develop visions and have capabilities for the future. We can say that a motivational conversion of the group is taking place if the time of indecision is seen as collective damage and if it is willing to converge towards a common denominator.

Reliability. In assemblies of participation and consultation, consecrated men and women often promise more than they can deliver. This is an underrated dimension in which the group's capital of reliability is at risk. Everyone is called to willingness, which translates into understanding and sharing through attitudes that are repeated and confirmed over time. This is how stable trust and co-operation arise.

55. In response to the decided signs of change taking place in consecrated life, we see nostalgic reactions, the repression of problems and resignation emerge. The time for opportunity is missed. We invite you to a renewed pedagogy of reliability. The decisions and choices are the near missionary future "capable of transforming everything".[46] They call upon us to work

[46] Francis, Apostolic Exhortation *Evangelii Gaudium* (24th November, 2013), 27.

together in the territories we are in. The creativity required by this new evangelisation will be the fruit of the Spirit who created charisms and can recreate them and make them living agents of evangelisation on communional journeys.

By itself, no religious institution can have the light and strength to deal with the complexity of today. The fecundity of the relationship between hierarchical and charismatic gifts is perceived: the Holy Spirit "brings about that wonderful communion of the faithful. He brings them into intimate union with Christ, so that he is the principle of the Church's unity".[47] The co-essentiality between the episcopate and charisms, and between the Petrine and Marian aspects, indicates to us another fundamental place of communion for the mission "with all those who in the Church are involved in the same undertaking, especially the Bishops".[48]

[47] CONGREGATION FOR THE DOCTRINE OF THE FAITH, Letter *Iuvenescit Ecclesia* to the Bishops of the Catholic Church Regarding the Relationship between Hierarchical and Charismatic Gifts in the Life and Mission of the Church (15th May, 2016), IV, 13.

[48] JOHN PAUL II, Post-Synodal Apostolic Exhortation *Vita Consecrata* (25th March, 1996), 81.

OUTSIDE THE GATES

One night Paul had a vision:
A Macedonian appeared and appealed to him in these words,
"Come across to Macedonia and help us".
Sailing from Troas we made a straight run for
Samothrace; the next day for Neapolis, and from there for
Philippi, a Roman colony and the principal city of that
particular district of Macedonia. After a few days in this
city we went along the river outside the gates as it was the
sabbath and this was a customary place for prayer.
We sat down and preached to the women
who had come to the meeting.
One of these women was called Lydia, a devout woman from
the town of Thyatira who was in the purple-dye trade.
She listened to us, and the Lord opened her heart to accept
what Paul was saying. After she and her household had
been baptised she sent us an invitation: "If you really think
me a true believer in the Lord", she said, "come and stay
with us"; and she would take no refusal.

(*Ac* 16:9, 11-15)

56. Holy Scripture offers us many possibilities to inspire, enlighten and guide the dynamic of *going forth* in our existence. We have chosen a page from the *Acts of the Apostles* (16:1-40): Apostle Paul's crossing into Macedonia. This is where the evangelisation of the world and cultures of the Roman Empire begins. It takes place during Paul's second missionary journey with Silas and Timothy. Let's take a closer look at the main events while underlining the most important aspects.

After the Council of Jerusalem and the solution of tensions in Antioch (cf. *Ac* 15:22-35), with the encouraging help of Judas and Silas, Barnabas and Paul stay in that community where they *taught and proclaimed the Good News, the word of the Lord* (*Ac* 15:35). Later, they decide to *go back and visit all the towns where they preached the word of the Lord* (*Ac* 15:36). However, a disagreement about Mark immediately interrupts their collaboration: Barnabas goes to Cyprus, and Paul goes towards Syria and Cilicia with Silas (*Ac* 15:39-41) and later, with Timothy as well.

In Asia Minor, they visit the communities founded on the first missionary journey and pass on the decisions reached by *the apostles and elders in Jerusalem* (*Ac* 16:4). But strangely, they are not able to travel inland: they are mysteriously *hindered* by the Spirit, the unpredictable protagonist. They decide to head north towards Troas. It is in this context that Paul has the vision during the night of a Macedonian who appeals: *Come across to Macedonia and help us!* (*Ac* 16:9). *Once he had seen this vision we lost no time in arranging a passage to Macedonia, convinced that God had called us to bring them the Good News* (*Ac* 16:10). It is perhaps a dream or a nightmare, but it is seen as a *call* that they answer, *losing no time* (*Ac* 16:10-11), by setting sail.

This is how the evangelisation of the European continent begins: with the city of Philippi which inhabited by Roman settlers and army veterans and has no stable synagogue or other organised religious structures. The preachers, who had relied upon the synagogues for the first proclamation, now find themselves forced to invent new opportunities for encounter.

57. *We went along the river outside the gates as it was the sabbath and this was a customary place for prayer. We sat down and preached to the women who had come to the meeting* (*Ac* 16:13). Being familiar with the religious practices and regulations of the time, the missionaries expect to find people *along the river, outside the gates*, or near the springs for the ritual ablutions. In fact, running water was necessary. No unusual signs can be seen, everything is normal: sitting, speaking and conversing with some of the women present. Paul, who had a rabbinic formation and had been taught to not waste time on women, must adapt: *We preached to the women who had come to the meeting* (*Ac* 16:13).

Familiar style, informal conversation: a seed sown in hope.

One of these women was called Lydia, a devout woman (*Ac* 16:14). Among the women present, there is a woman who works in the purple-dye trade, Lydia of Thyatira, a city known for its textile production and which is also mentioned in the *Book of Revelation* (cf. *Rv* 1:11, 2:18-19). This woman is open to the Jewish religious values: the text says *seboménê ton Theòn, worshiper/devout woman of God* (v. 14; cf. 13:43, 10:2). Luke likes to point out as examples certain people who are at the *threshold* of faith: Lydia is "listening" (present continuous) with her friends to what Paul is saying.

The Lord opened her heart to accept what Paul was saying (*Ac* 16:14). The initiative for the conversation, in the sincere willingness of an attentive heart, comes from the Lord; it is he who opens the heart up to faith, kindles it and convinces it (cf. *Lk* 24:45). God's action is expressed using bold words: the Greek verb (*diènoixen*) refers to the dilation of a woman's uterus so that life can be born. For Lydia, who was already *a devout woman*, it means letting herself be led to life in full, "coming to the light", "leaving the womb". Also, the verb *to adhere* (*prosékein*) indicates to hold on to, to seize, to find solidity. Lydia reaches the *solid ground* of faith, stable maturity.

58. *After she and her household had been baptised she sent us an invitation: "If you really think me a true believer in the Lord", she said, "come and stay with us"; and she would take no refusal* (*Ac* 16:15). The hospitality that Lydia insists on offering to the missionaries confirms the fullness of her adhesion to the faith. The woman feels that it is her duty to

put into practice what she has accepted and what she is learning: to share one's possessions. Thus, her house becomes a place of meeting and prayer.

Paul, who is attached to his autonomy schema, is "compelled" to accept a serious change in method (cf. *Ac* 18:3; *1 Th* 2:9; *2 Th* 3:8; *1 Co* 4:12; 9:13-15; *Ph* 4:15-16). The word forced us (*parabiàsato*) [to stay] (v. 15) also refers to this. Lydia, *charmed* by God and *given life*, now charms and instils strength: welcoming prevails.

59. Let's look briefly at the development of this community founded on prayer. *While they were going to prayer* (v. 16) a slave-girl, who was a soothsayer and exploited by her masters, kept following Paul and his friends, shouting to everyone that those foreign men were servants of the *Most High God* (v. 18). Paul loses his temper and drives the spirit of divination out of her. In doing this, he ruins the business of the woman's exploiters who then begin spreading word that the new preachers are subverting religious practices. The magistrates believe them without making many inquiries; they have the missionaries flogged and put into prison.

Despite the suffering and injustice, Paul, Barnabas and Timothy continue *singing God's praises, while the other prisoners listened* (v. 25). While they are praying, there is a kind of earthquake; the chains fall and all the doors fly open. The gaoler, awakened by the event, thinks the prisoners are escaping and wants to kill himself. Paul reassures him, and the gaoler begins caring for the prisoners and washing their wounds, in the end agreeing to be baptised with his household and offering to host the celebration at his home (vv. 26-34). Paul discovers friends and disciples where he least expected. Another family becomes a protagonist in the construction of the community at Philippi, which is built, beyond any plan or expectation, between the house of a matron and a gaoler. The next day, Paul is set free. Although an injustice had been committed against him as a Roman citizen, *civis romanus*, it is prudent for him to leave the city: *They came and begged them to leave leave the town* (v. 39). But first, Paul passes by Lydia's house; he meets the brothers and they encourage each other before he leaves for Thessalonika (v. 40). The missionary adventure continues.

60. Agreeing to be hosted at Lydia's house free of charge, which had been a forced decision, becomes a providential resource. Paul will continue to

pay special attention to the community at Philippi: as his Letter to the *Philippians* reveals. He will learn of their developments and crises from Timothy and receives support for his work only from them (cf. *Ph* 4:15-16). Apart from his nostalgia and affection, he gives them an extraordinary Christological hymn (*Ph* 2:6-11), interpreting the sentiments with which he had been welcomed and helped. We can draw many inspiring values from this episode that can guide us in our situations and missionary adventures.

61. Without a doubt, Philippi was an unknown and a risk, but if one knows how to read God's signs - the vision of the Macedonian in the night is seen as a *call from God* (cf. v. 10) - he can see new opportunities that call to explore new lands. The lack of stable institutions sharpens the imagination, and missionaries sense where to find someone to start with: *along the river outside the gates* (v. 13). Paul sows by improvising, but it is the Lord who opens hearts to the adherence of faith and who inspires certain *forced actions*: *constraint* is fruit of Lydia's generosity, but also of her coherence with the practised faith. Two families are involved in this first adventure: the family of the rich and bold matron and that of the gaoler, a man accustomed to abuse and transformed by the surprise of grace in witness of acts of tenderness and generosity.

Difficulties, risks and wounds have become symbols and mediations of newness, which are only later understood. It is a challenge to break the mould, an exercise of faith and communion with no guarantees or definite resources. This was a transition into maturity with human wisdom, but also with *parrhesia* and boldness, which allowed new paths to the Gospel to open in a different culture and with different protagonists.

62. *Going outside the gates* remains a symbol of all of the *goings forth* of our Founders and Foundresses who we remember, praising their courage and genius. We have learned how to remember the fragile experiences, the conditions of poverty and unjust suffering and the risky improvisations experienced in our origins by Founders and Foundresses. It is not only about the moving memory, we cannot reduce everything to *golden legends*, but about recovering the state of invention and charism *in statu nascenti*. Opportunities that we must always recover and experience, with boldness, but also with concrete willingness. Even a nightmare can reveal itself to be a "call" from God!

IN THE MINDSET THAT GENERATES AND TRANSFORMS

63. Paul's apostolic journey outlines a new geography of Christian proclamation. The missionaries, who are prepared to change direction according to the compass of the Spirit, follow a path that leads from Jerusalem to new territories, cultures and peoples. They cross Phrygia, Galatia, Mysia, Bithynia and travel to Troas, they try to travel to Macedonia, sail towards Samothrace and Neapolis, and arrive in Philippi. They stay there, but they do not stop. There is another path to take: the one that leads from the gates of the city along the river.

Paul and Silas inhabit the world in the sign of real encounter and ferial conversation, in everyday places where life is spent without false idealities and where it regenerates. Pope Francis invites us to experience reality: "We have politicians - and even religious leaders - who wonder why people do not understand and follow them, since their proposals are so clear and logical. Perhaps it is because they are stuck in the realm of pure ideas and end up reducing politics or faith to rhetoric. Others have left simplicity behind and have imported a rationality foreign to most people".[1] Paul and Silas meet men and women in places where life flows with its baggage from work, anxiety, feelings and desires, and tell them of the passion that inhabits them. This inner vision does not fear discussion and concreteness; it becomes a new mindset that is capable of generating new horizons and new opportunities and therefore, capable of acting and transforming. It becomes generative movement.

PEDAGOGY OF SECULARITY

64. The secularity of culture, which will degrade in secularisation, poses a question that is still valid today for theological reflection, for witness and Christian proclamation and especially, for formation to mission. We could say it is a pedagogy of secularity, that is, an attention in which the entire person educates himself to experience the world with a Christian soul, searching for the creative mark that God has left on him. This process, which we can define as a process of wisdom and as generative of

---

[1] Francis, Apostolic Exhortation *Evangelii Gaudium* (24th November, 2013), 232.

evangelical life, should be part of the formation of consecrated men and women according to their specific form of life.

In *Evangelii Gaudium*, the following question is quietly present: Is secularity, a complex and contradictory phenomenon, unrelated and opposed to Christian faith, or on the contrary, is it consistent with its essence? The Church recognises the secular entity of the world entrusted by God to man's responsibility. At the same time, the Church exists in open solidarity with it, not to make it sacred, but to make it the seed of sanctification. Experiencing the world, therefore, is an archetype to combine the prophetic mission of the Church with. According to the doctrine of *Gaudium et Spes* which talks about a legitimate secularity of society, worldly and profane realities have their own autonomy and reason for being. "For by the very circumstance of their having been created, all things are endowed with their own stability, truth, goodness, proper laws and order".[2] Deeper involvement in the secular world can be a way to God because "earthly matters and the concerns of faith derive from the same God. Indeed whoever labours to penetrate the secrets of reality with a humble and steady mind, even though he is unaware of the fact, is nevertheless being led by the hand of God, who holds all things in existence, and gives them their identity".[3]

65. Mission requires delicate balance: co-determining the path of the secular world without wanting to determine it.[4] The Church, Pope Francis affirms, "stands by people every step of the way", no matter how difficult or lengthy this may prove to be. It is familiar with patient expectation and apostolic endurance" while it "consists mostly of patience and disregard for constraints of time".[5]

The Word was the true light that enlightens all men; and he was coming into the world. He was in the world that had its being through him, and the world did not know him (*Jn* 1:9-10): this Word is fulfilled

[2] Vatican II Ecumenical Council, Pastoral Constitution on the Church in the Modern World *Gaudium et Spes* (7th December, 1965), 36.

[3] *Idem.*

[4] Cf. K. Rahner, *Riflessioni Teologiche sulla Secolarizzazione e sull'Ateismo*, in *Nuovi Saggi* IV, Paoline, Rome 19641985, 244-257.

[5] Francis, Apostolic Exhortation *Evangelii Gaudium* (24th November, 2013), 24.

in secular conditions. The paradigm of the theology of God in the world, incarnation, can only be expressed through secular categories.

Secularity has been indicated as "the proper and specific character" of that form of consecrated life incarnated in secular institutes.[6] Today, the relationship with the world interpellates all forms of consecrated life in every dimension: our existence and our attitudes of dialogue, witness and mission. Paul walks out of the gates and along the river; he immerses himself in secularity, confronting his faith and allowing the meeting to educate him in the newness of the Spirit. The Church is called to enter into this hermeneutical process to witness the effort of the search and the bliss of a beyond: "The human experience is not only an experience of this and that, an experience well-defined in its contents, but it is an experience of the finiteness that leads to an infinite horizon".[7]

66. Passion makes us friends with life and friends with men, part of humanity that dream of a more just and fraternal future. It is nice to think about a consecrated man in a secular institute who turned his work in the world into a missionary song: "Our 'programme' of sanctification has been upset; we believed that the silent walls of prayer were sufficient! We believed that closed within the internal fortress of prayer we could stay apart from the problems that were troubling the world; [...] a situation that tells us that Jesus's cry: *go and proclaim the Good News to every creature*, or rather *take up your cross and follow me* is not a mere expression of piety. We have to change society! [...] we have to get involved, sharpen our tools; we need reflection, culture, word, work, etc., as well as ploughs to plough the field of new effort and weapons to fight our battle of transformation and love. We must transform the flawed structures of the human city; repair the ruined houses of man, according to the principal commandment of charity".[8] Such incarnation becomes a formative necessity, a continuous pedagogy to implement without considering it in any way fulfilled.

---

[6] PIUS XII, *Motu Proprio Primo Feliciter* (12th March, 1948), 5.

[7] K. RAHNER, cit., in R. GIBELLINI, *La Teologia del XX Secolo*, Queriniana, Brescia 2007, 241.

[8] G. LA PIRA, *Le città sono vive*, La Scuola, Brescia 2005.

THE GENERATIONAL RELATIONSHIP

67. The crisis of the relationships and communication between generations is a significant phenomenon of our time. The widespread confusion regarding identity, age, role and feelings that conditions the exchange between generations defines our society as adolescentric. The crisis we are experiencing in relationships at every level is closely related to the concept of personal freedom. The personalist principle of conditional freedom was replaced by the permissive principle of unconditional freedom, which today is understood as the simple possibility to do something, as opposed to the possibility to choose to do something. We are experiencing a crisis of proposed values: there are no references to the fundamental rules shaped on the nature of human beings.

The young men and women that we welcome with us in the 'sequela' of Christ and in mission are the post-modern generation. Their experience gives us questions. All of us, but especially young people, are the result of cultural processes at work; in particular, the idea of the individual who is debased, deprived of the substantiality that philosophers and theologians attributed to him up until the modern age. This nihilistic premise creates a man who is deprived of his individuality and who is replicated in multiple identities suited to a wide range of situations. The young generation does not know how to describe their malaise; they experience, with unperceived suffering, emotional illiteracy that keeps them from recognising their own feelings.

68. The new digital culture, this culture that invades personal, collective and social spaces, accelerates these processes. It contributes to the mixing of beliefs, opinions, trends and choices, challenging people, agencies and designated places to instill knowledge and values, the Church included. "The means of social communication", as Saint John Paul II writes in his encyclical *Redemptoris Missio* in 1990, "have become so important as to be for many the chief means of information and education, of guidance and inspiration in their behaviour as individuals, families and within society at large. In particular, the younger generation is growing up in a world conditioned by the mass media".[9] Through technology,

[9] JOHN PAUL II, Encyclical Letter *Redemptoris Missio* (7th December, 1990), 37.

codes of transmission and languages, the new digital culture builds up and tears down man's identity, his ages and the idea of the world, in an unresolvable crisis. The forms and figures of social relationships are redefined. The processes of mental construction and representations of the world, in other words, the very idea of reality, are reset. The digital culture that makes available to us and connects us to infinite possibilities of information and relationships opens up, with clear ambivalence, to the deconstruction of the social bonds that our identities are founded on. We go about without values and without points of reference, incapable of communication between generations and genders, creating imaginary and fictitious worlds.

69. The generational crisis becomes a generative provocation to construct real places where, in the sign of encounter, we can grow in the responsibility of the world and in it, ecclesial mission: "Every generation has the task of engaging anew in the arduous search for the right way to order human affairs; this task is never simply completed. Yet every generation must also make its own contribution to establishing convincing structures of freedom and of good, which can help the following generation as a guideline for the proper use of human freedom; hence, always within human limits, they provide a certain guarantee also for the future".[10] Benedict XVI points out a problem which is at the centre of international debate: intergenerational responsibility.

We invite you to accompany young consecrated men and women by creating bonds of knowledge and affection. They "call us to renewed and expansive hope, for they represent new directions for humanity and open us up to the future, lest we cling to a nostalgia for structures and customs which are no longer life-giving in today's world".[11] Constant listening and frank dialogue between generations becomes a place for encounter between the provocations of the modern world and consecrated life, a hermeneutical and creative space for new methods and languages. A pedagogy of man and his mystery of relationship: "It is helpful to listen to young people and the elderly. Both represent a source of hope for every people. The elderly bring with them memory and the wisdom

---

[10] BENEDICT XVI, Encyclical Letter *Spe Salvi* (30th November, 2007), 25.

[11] FRANCIS, Apostolic Exhortation *Evangelii Gaudium* (24th November, 2013), 108.

of experience, which warns us not to foolishly repeat our past mistakes. Young people call us to renewed and expansive hope, for they represent new directions for humanity and open us up to the future, lest we cling to a nostalgia for structures and customs which are no longer life-giving in today's world".[12]

COMPARISON WITH REALITY

70. We are invited to experience the world with a commitment to encounter, to enter into relation with. Reality is structured through meaningful relationships and interactions and guiding values. Today, there is talk about meaningful relationality that does not exhaust with family bonds, but rather expands to the point of creating a universal bond. It is through this mindset that John Paul II won over young people, communicating commitment and hope, and that Pope Francis invites to a dynamic reality towards the most distant peripheries which he brings from the margins and unknown fringes of the world back to the centre and beyond in planetary harmony: "We need to pay attention to the global so as to avoid narrowness and banality. Yet we also need to look to the local, which keeps our feet on the ground".[13] This prevents polarisation. People can live "in an abstract, globalised universe, falling into step behind everyone else, admiring the glitter of other people's world, gaping and applauding at all the right times" or they can become "a museum of local folklore, a world apart, doomed to doing the same things over and over, and incapable of being challenged by novelty or appreciating the beauty which God bestows beyond their borders".[14]

71. Pope Francis continues, "What calls us to action are realities illuminated by reason. Formal nominalism has to give way to harmonious objectivity. Otherwise, the truth is manipulated, cosmetics take the place of real care for our bodies".[15] And, "we constantly have to broaden our horizons and see the greater good which will benefit us all. But this has to

---

[12] *Idem.*

[13] *Ibid.*, 234.

[14] *Idem.*

[15] *Ibid.*, 232.

be done without evasion or uprooting. We need to sink our roots deeper into the fertile soil and history of our native place, which is a gift of God. We can work on a small scale, in our own neighbourhood, but with a larger perspective".[16]

72. Reality requires creative conversion so that we are not giving answers to questions that no one is asking, thereby leaving the existential questions of men and women today without adequate answers; the ways of proclamation must be reinvented. Creativity, and the boldness that it requires, makes us *watchmen of the morning* (cf. *Is* 21:11), capable of risking, of "abandon[ing] the complacent attitude that says: 'We have always done it this way'",[17] of "rethinking the goals, structures, style and methods of evangelisation in their respective communities".[18]

Rethinking the structures will sometimes lead to taking existing structures, that are no longer suitable for transmitting the beauty of the Good News, out of consideration.[19] Renewing the language is urgent for the comprehension of the Gospel. Putting the Gospel, the Church's Magisterium, into words, images and symbols that are meaningful in contemporary cultures is an arduous task even because of the limited Christian memory many of our people have: few concepts and the absolute lack of framework. The patterns and customs that we speak with and through which we show the identity and values of consecrated life risk being hermetic and incomprehensible for most people. Pope Francis says, "I hope that all communities will devote the necessary effort to advancing along the path of a pastoral and missionary conversion".[20]

PLURAL CONVERSION

73. Throughout the centuries, consecrated life has been one of the realities of the Church that has had to face cultural diversities more than the others: it cannot stop today. The path of conversion that calls upon consecrated life to create fruitful relationships continues.

---

[16] *Ibid.*, 235.

[17] *Ibid.*, 33.

[18] *Idem.*

[19] Cf. *Ibid.*, 27.

[20] *Ibid.*, 25.

"It is easy to realise how strong the bond is that unites the Church's mission with the culture and cultures".[21] Interpreting the Gospel requires cultural decentralisation. Is living the Gospel in the encounter with cultures a path that can renew consecrated life? *Perfectae Caritatis* invited us to a movement of updating. This led to greater familiarity with the world, in particular with the poor and marginalised, and evangelical simplicity. Today, the intercultural reality demands that we continue this renewal. Evangelisation cannot occur without a respectful approach to cultures, just like contact with cultures cannot occur without the abandoning of the self in the name of the Gospel. The future thus calls us to two tensions: stability and changes, it calls us to be a place of interaction between the particular and the universal.

We are invited to learn the difficult art of relating with the different and of cordial collaboration to build together. Solitary commitments and efforts have no future because they exclude us from the mystery of the Church as *communion*. *Koinonìa* is strengthened in the plurality in which *God's comprehensive wisdom* (*Ep* 3:10) shines.

This is the great conversion that provokes us in practical choices as well. "I also hope for a growth in communion between the members of different Institutes". Pope Francis invites us to go forth "more courageously from the confines of our respective Institutes and to work together, at the local and global levels, on projects involving formation, evangelisation, and social action. This would make for a more effective prophetic witness. No one contributes to the future in isolation, by his or her efforts alone, but by seeing himself or herself as part of a true communion which is constantly open to encounter, dialogue, attentive listening and mutual assistance. Such a communion inoculates us from the disease of self-absorption. Consecrated men and women are also called to true synergy with all other vocations in the Church, beginning with priests and the lay faithful, in order to 'spread the spirituality of communion, first of all in their internal life and then in the ecclesial community, and even beyond its boundaries'".[22]

---

[21] JOHN PAUL II, *Message* to Italian Bishops gathered in a General Assembly in Collevalenza (11th November, 1996).

[22] FRANCIS, Apostolic Letter *To all Consecrated People on the Occasion of the Year of Consecrated Life* (21st November, 2014), IV, 3.

WITH THE PERIPHERIES IN THE HEART

74. The consecrated life is called to carry out its mission in new ways and in new contexts, *outside the gates and along the river* (cf. *Ac* 16:13). We feel called to be present, for evangelical election, in situations of misery and oppression, doubt and discomfort, fear and loneliness, to show that God's tenderness and his grief for the suffering of his children know no limits.

Jesus invites us to go beyond, to take chances on new paths, to collaborate with every man of good will to care for and watch over the seed of his Word so that it grows strong. This means coming out of indifference; it means bringing those who have been discarded from humanity's journey out of anonymity and humiliation; it means not letting comforts, prejudices or presumptuous improvisation have control over us. Ultimately, it means assuming the deepest humanity, as Jesus Christ did. Paul and his friends did it by inventing new ways of reaching the women and men of their time, living with them in the ordinariness of life.

IN THE OUTPOSTS

75."The Church must step outside herself. To go where? To the outskirts of existence, whatever they may be, but she must step out. Jesus tells us: Go into all the world! Go! Preach! Bear witness to the Gospel (cf. *Mk* 16:15)".[23] One of the characteristics of Pope Francis's magisterium is the invitation to shape a Church that goes forth, in a manner of mercy, nearness and solidarity, being careful not to surrender to intimism and giving ourselves the people, active and responsible, with the oil of hope and consolation, of every fragility and unrest, disappointment and joy. "It is a hermeneutical question: reality is understood only if it is looked at from the periphery [...] we need to move away from the central position of calmness and peacefulness and direct ourselves to the peripheral areas. Being at the periphery helps to see and to understand better".[24]

Immersing ourselves in Pope Francis's polyhedral mindset gives us another opportunity to look at reality from the peripheries. One constant

[23] Francis, *Address* of the Holy Father on the Occasion of Vigil of Pentecost with the Ecclesial Movements, le Nuove Comunità, le Associazioni e le Aggregazioni Laicali (18th May, 2013).

[24] A. Spadaro, *"Wake Up the World!" Conversation with Pope Francis on Religious Life*, in *La Civiltà Cattolica*, 165 (2014/I), 6.

of consecrated life has always been its presence in the frontiers, all the way to the outposts of the mission, assuming the greatest risks with courage and genius.[25] Today, during this time of epochal change, we are called to the same thing. Looking at reality from the peripheries is also the courage to face new challenges, try new ways, to play a part in "elaborating and putting into effect new initiatives of evangelisation for present-day situations".[26] We must know how to sense and "to create 'alternate spaces', where the Gospel approach of selfgiving, fraternity, embracing differences, and love of one another can thrive".[27]

76. Pope Francis continues to ask us to wake up the world through our life and ministry,[28] accepting with boldness, compassion, and ever-renewed genius, the risk of new people who are not chosen for one's own convenience, but are found through exploring new geographical, cultural, social and existential peripheries, in the rejects of history and of globalised indifference, among the thousands of figures of disfigured faces and crushed dignity. Let's reread our Letter *Keep Watch* and its urgent call to discernment and to move forward towards disregarded horizons.[29] These human places, which at times go unvisited, call to missionary conversion: *He has sent me to bring the Good News to the poor, to proclaim liberty to captives and to the blind new sight, to set the downtrodden free, to proclaim the Lord's year of favour* (*Lk* 4:18-19).

WALKING WITH THE POOR

77. We are called to *act justly, to love tenderly and to walk humbly with our God* (*Mi* 6:8). Consecrated men and women are always on the front lines defending threatened life, proposing another possible and necessary way

---

[25] Cf. Paul VI, Apostolic Exhortation *Evangelii Nuntiandi* (8th December, 1975), 69; John Paul II, Post-Synodal Apostolic Exhortation *Vita Consecrata* (25th March, 1996), 76.

[26] John Paul II, Post-Synodal Apostolic Exhortation *Vita Consecrata* (25th March, 1996), 73.

[27] Francis, Apostolic Letter *To all Consecrated People on the Occasion of the Year of Consecrated Life* (21st November, 2014), II, 2.

[28] A. Spadaro, *"Wake Up the World!" Conversation with Pope Francis on Religious Life*, in *La Civiltà Cattolica*, 165 (2014/I).

[29] Congregation for Institutes of Consecrated Life and Societies of Apostolic Life, *Keep Watch To Consecrated Men and Women Journeying in the Footsteps of God* (8th September, 2014), LEV, Vatican City 2014.

of living. Few things evoke admiration, surprise and interest like seeing consecrated men and women beside people who have nothing, beside those who are considered to be the last, the rejects of society, and they go where others do not want to be. The preferential option for the poor that configured the life and mission of Jesus (*Lk* 4:18) is one of the basic principles guiding discernment in the Orders, Congregations and Institutes of consecrated life and the Societies of Apostolic life. All of us are asked to have attention that goes beyond sociological analysis and to invoke passion and compassion. "Serving the poor is an act of evangelisation and, at the same time, a seal of Gospel authenticity and a catalyst for permanent conversion in the consecrated life, since, as Saint Gregory the Great says, 'when charity lovingly stoops to provide even for the smallest needs of our neighbour, then does it suddenly surge upwards to the highest peaks. And when in great kindness it bends to the most extreme needs, then with much vigour does it resume its soaring to the heights'".[30]

The *familiaritas cum pauperibus* has always been the feature of every new "beginning" and reform. "Solidarity [...] is not a feeling of vague compassion or shallow distress at the misfortunes of so many people, both near and far. On the contrary, it is a firm and persevering determination to commit oneself to the common good; that is to say to the good of all and of each individual, because we are all really responsible for all".[31]

FOR AN INTEGRAL AND SOLIDARY HUMANISM

78. A prophetic sign is composed of a new lifestyle into which we work to integrate justice, peace and the safeguarding of creation. Pope Francis reminds us in the Encyclical Letter *Laudato si'*: "An awareness of the gravity of today's cultural and ecological crisis must be translated into new habits. Many people know that our current progress and the mere amassing of things and pleasures are not enough to give meaning and joy to the human heart, yet they feel unable to give up what the market sets before them".[32] This commitment at the personal and community levels, connected with all of the organisations that work to bring these Gospel

[30] JOHN PAUL II, Post-Synodal Apostolic Exhortation *Vita Consecrata* (25th March, 1996), 82.

[31] JOHN PAUL II, Encyclical Letter *Sollicitudo Rei Socialis* (30th December, 1987), 38.

[32] FRANCIS, Encyclical Letter *Laudato Si'* (18th June, 2015), 209.

values to life, allows us to promote an integral and solidary humanism. Our lifestyles, in the various forms of consecration, have the strength to oppose the paradigms of the dominant culture and the economistic concept that everything is measured by the parameters of productive income and profit in the logic of the market. They are able to represent a real alternative to the culture of waste, in the dynamism of gratuitousness and solidarity, out of respect for otherness and in the sense of mystery, open to the unpredictable and to what cannot be planned. We must recognise their beneficial choice of austerity and the refusal of wastage by communities and individuals. This allows us to escape the dynamics of consumerism that create the incapacity to distinguish true needs from those needs which are purely induced and from the mere exploitation of nature. In this fragmented world, which is incapable of making definitive choices and is characterised by many different levels of uncertainty, the totality of our belonging to God becomes a hospitable place for humanity and all of creation. Contemplation, devotion and fecundity, and prophetic witness are missionary experience for an integral humanism.

FOR NON-VIOLENT ACTION

79. In *Octogesima Adveniens*, Pope Paul VI affirmed: "It is not enough to recall principles, state intentions, point to crying injustice and utter prophetic denunciations; these words will lack real weight unless they are accompanied for each individual by a livelier awareness of personal responsibility and by effective action".[33]

Many consecrated men and women are called to live out their missions in areas under serious threats of violence and terrorism, of the recrudescence of religious and idealogical fundamentalism, of exploitation of the environment and sensitivity towards other situations and forms of human conflict, often giving their lives to the point of martyrdom. We are called to open our hearts to make room for the people who do not share our faith, our values and our culture.

At the heart of this encounter is common commitment, in a culture of respect, tolerance, reconciliation and peace, but also collaboration in protecting those who are weakest, in particular, women and children, in prevention and in guaranteeing adequate punishment for the guilty. We

[33] PAUL VI, Apostolic Letter *Octogesima Adveniens* (14th May, 1971), 48.

must develop and exercise our creative capacity: propose alternatives, create horizons, imagine possible worlds. We must be capable of an action that is lucid and a bearer of hope to the disenchanted and open to the future, critical and vital, seeing the real and imagining the future, in order to echo today the paradoxical word that is the Good News when it proclaims that the last will be first, those who mourn are blessed and death is overcome.

IN THE EVERYDAY OF FAMILY

80. To begin the Year of Consecrated Life, Pope Francis stressed: "I thank the Lord that the Year of Consecrated Life coincides with the Synod on the Family. Family life and consecrated life are both vocations which bring enrichment and blessings for all. They are spaces where human growth comes about through relationships, and they are also places of evangelisation.

Each can help the other".[34] Family and consecrated life recognise themselves in the freedom of the Spirit and in the communion of the Church: this joyous confession is daily support in the common journey of devotion.

The Holy Father reminds us again that the families we encounter daily "with their faces, their stories, with all their complications are not a problem, they are an opportunity that God places before us. An opportunity that challenges us to generate a missionary creativity capable of embracing every practical situation [...] Not only those that come or that are in the parishes - this would be easy, more or less –, but being able to go to the families of our districts, to those who do not come". Our capacity for nearness and boldness "compels us to go beyond the declaration of principles so as to enter into the beating heart of neighbourhoods and, as artisans, setting ourselves to mould God's dream in this reality, something that can be done only by people of faith, those who do not close access to the action of the Spirit, and who get their hands dirty".[35]

[34] FRANCIS, Apostolic Letter *To all Consecrated People on the Occasion of the Year of Consecrated Life* (21st November, 2014), III, 2.

[35] FRANCIS, *Address* at the opening of the Pastoral Congress of the Diocese of Rome (16th June, 2016), 1. Paul and his friends will meet Lydia's hospitable family who will accompany them with their generosity along the missionary journey. They will also meet the gaoler's family who becomes a sign of hospitality and solidarity for them (cf. *Ac* 16:13-15, 25-34).

ON EDUCATIONAL FRONTIERS

81. The Church is a narrating community that represents God's love in Jesus Christ. Such narration is essentially educational.

STRUCK BY HER TEACHING

The manifestation of Christ's mystery concerns the whole of human life in all of its areas, and it aims to bring every man and the whole man to a new way of being and living (*Ac* 22:8-10). A consistent Western tradition defined the educational process as the progressive directing of the person towards complete self-realisation. The Church embraced this idea with a new hermeneutic. The mission of the Church can therefore be properly considered in pedagogical categories: *my children! I must go through the pain of giving birth to you all over again, until Christ is formed in you* (*Ga* 4:19).

The believer perceives the inner logic of the life of faith and understands the educational dimension of its humanity. The connection between the Christian message and the educational experience leads to the development of a pedagogical doctrine. Not from doctrine to life, but from life to doctrine.

Consecrated life in its many forms has been an educational agent throughout human and Church history, and it is called to continue on this journey with genius and dialogue with the world. We cannot limit our missionary presence, vision and charity to only the first relief of indigence, but with brave competence we must fulfil the Church's proper educational task. It is a contribution that we cannot disregard, in the life of the Church or in civil society.

82. The educational task throughout our mission questions our way of looking at and experiencing existential peripheries and our way of providing them with company, relief, merciful encounter and embrace. We must direct personal stories of faith to an educative encounter. We must accompany and shed light on the doubts that torment, and the shadows and fears that block.

We are called to the indispensable pedagogical path that the Church has always followed in the world, watching Jesus the Master with the humility of the disciples: *He taught in their synagogues and everyone praised him; they were astonished by the gracious words that came from his lips. He taught them on the sabbath. And his teaching made a deep impression on them because he spoke with authority* (*Lk* 4:15, 22,31,32). Our every missionary and diaconal action affirms or denies the educational act: it encounters the story of every person, doubts, faith, opacity and beauty. Educating Christ's way resounds as a prophetic task that the Church entrusts to us: "*Recalling and serving the divine plan for humanity*, as it is announced in Scripture and as it emerges from an attentive reading of the signs of God's providential action in history".[36]

IN THE CULTURAL PERIPHERIES

83. The service of knowledge, the diakonia of culture, calls us to new and fruitful work of making faith culturally responsible in order to revitalise, in a critical and creative way, the old and dialectical relationship between faith and culture. Peter Hans Kolvenbach, former Super General of the Jesuits, affirmed in his intervention at the 12th General Assembly of the Synod on consecrated life: some consecrated persons assume, in a more special way, this ecclesial mission to remind cultures of their ultimate goal; they work in the very heart of these cultures, in their places of research or artistic creation, in academic institutions and diffusion centres of the means of social communication.

Vita Consecrata highlighted this point: "The need to contribute to the promotion of culture and to the dialogue between culture and faith is deeply felt in the Church today. Consecrated persons cannot fail to feel challenged by this pressing need".[37] We remember in particular the consecrated persons and Institutes called by the Spirit to become interpreters of the great educational narration in contemporary cultures. We invite you to not abandon the inclination to the educational that is so necessary in the weak culture of today, in the culture of fragments, in the fictitious constructions of the virtual and in the unstoppable flow of *anything goes*.

[36] John Paul II, Post-Synodal Apostolic Exhortation *Vita Consecrata* (25th March, 1996), 73.
[37] *Ibid*., 98a; b.

84. Today, in the peripheries of culture, consecrated life, in line with the old and fruitful *traditio* - in respectful and sympathetic dialogue with all cultural agents - is called to engage on two fronts: experiential and speculative. The first invites us to live our witness of life in the furrow of the Gospel narrative, which is possible at any age and in every period of life. The story gives life to the educational act and introduces into the actuality of the encounter with Christ.

The second calls us to deep reflection on contemporary man for an integral humanism. This prophetic challenge requires the dedication of intelligence, passion, intuition and resources. The Church needs to have contexts, spaces, and forms of education that help the deep freedom of the person to achieve a movement that is symmetrical to that of the cultures of consumption: the generative movement.

FOR A FORMATIVE EMBRACE

85. We invite you to recover the attitude of imitating Jesus the Master through the humble service of culture and discernment in relation with the Truth, extended to all aspects of human life.

We currently sense that many adults have stopped giving new generations reasons and rules for living with freedom and responsibility. Reawakening their binding educational responsibility is valuable to all areas where consecrated persons are present.

We can also rethink our willingness to offer places and environments of reference and belonging, tangible spaces of human sharing in the face of emergency of situations, even dramatic ones, of loneliness and uncertainty, places that are capable of meeting the needs of friendship, experimentation and discussion to help not only children and young people, but even adults, to overcome their narcissistic concentration on themselves. The challenge, therefore, of proclaiming to today's man the wreckage of loneliness and the Good News of the founding relationship with the Mystery of God that reveals itself as Love, is decisive. In this perspective, there is a need today for creative planning, a need to research and to try new paths.

We also invite you to focus your attention on the plurality of educational contexts: the plural guiding values, cultural belongings, ways of family life, educational figures, knowledge and sources of knowledge. We must know how to recognise new educational and pastoral opportunities and the knots that these phenomena bring with them, and understand that we are asked to make effort to find new paths of educational unity within the plurality. This requires the launch of new educational professionalism, in addition to traditional professionalism, because the potentialities offered by pluralisation (migrants, increase in cultural minorities, multiculturality of scholastic curriculums, new demands on proclamation and catechesis) risk remaining unfulfilled or spent only on emergencies of social services. The Church community and consecrated life itself will accommodate these new needs by developing a new educational commitment.

IN ECUMENICAL AND INTER-RELIGIOUS PLACES

86. We invite you to read the phenomenon of migration that requires new pastoral awareness and attention from us regarding ecumenism and inter-religious dialogue.

Vita Consecrata provides very concrete indications: the sharing of the *lectio divina*, participation in common prayer, dialogue of friendship and charity, "cordial hospitality shown to brothers and sisters of the various Christian confessions, mutual knowledge and the exchange of gifts, co-operation in common undertakings of service and of witness: these are among the many forms of ecumenical dialogue [...] No Institute of Consecrated Life should feel itself dispensed from working for this cause".[38]

No less is required of us to foster inter-religious dialogue. Two fields can inspire our practical response: "The shared *concern for human life*, extending from compassion for those who are suffering physically and spiritually to commitment to justice, peace and the protection of God's creation. In these areas, Institutes of active life especially will seek an understanding with members of other religions, through that 'dialogue of action' which prepares the way for more profound exchanges. A particular field for successful common action with people of other religious traditions is that of *efforts to promote the dignity of women*. In view of the equality and authentic complementarity of men and women, a valuable service can be rendered above all by consecrated women".[39]

---

[38] *Ibid.*, 101.

[39] *Ibid.*, 102.

87. We invite you to revisit the old forms that monks and nuns, men and women religious, and all consecrated persons gave life to in an attempt to actualise an alternative project of society and the creation of places in which living the Gospel gives meaning and direction and becomes living witness of fraternity that knows how to encounter cultures and peoples.

The sign of evangelical novelty can expand across broader structures of evangelisation: places of pilgrimage, often supported or animated by consecrated men and women, are spaces of conversion and contemplation; monasteries are places of welcome and dialogue that are open to ecumenism and also to non-believers who often rediscover the meaning of life inside. Consecrated life, which, in the past, knew how to create and manage works inspired by the logic of the Gospel, is today called to rethink, reinvent, and recreate places where the Gospel can be read in its possibilities, inspirations and fruits, and where one can see and touch God.

Luigia Tincani, Foundress of an apostolic religious institute, writes, "Along our common journey towards the full age of the children of God, all that I can do for my brothers is just, ultimately, make myself living matter in which they can see the idea that I would like to see flourish in their journey realised. This is so education can be seen as the true art and poetry of life. The only thing I can do is offer them the consistency of my mind, my heart, my actions and my words, as the artist offers the work in which he has put the living thrill of his art. Because the truth is this: we can only do good around us, we can only be educators, for merit of our moral value, for the strength of our convictions, for the reality of actualisation that our ideal moral reaches within us. Therefore, if we want to become educators, it is more important to concern ourselves with bringing these desired ideals to life within ourselves, rather than in other people".[40]

[40] L. Tincani, *Lettere di Formazione*, edited by C. Broggi, Studium, Rome 2009 (1923).

IN THE TIME OF HOPE

THE CHURCH IS HERE

88. At the beginning of these pages, we heard to the promise that resonates in the Acts: *You will receive the power when the Holy Spirit comes on you, and then you will be my witnesses not only in Jerusalem but throughout Judea and Samaria, and indeed to the ends of the earth* (*Ac* 1:8). Jesus entrusts his last message to the word *witnesses*. For the apostles, being witnesses means having been with the Lord, having participated in his passion and resurrection. Witness does not come to them through a personal decision. It is God who chose them and who sent the Spirit to make them capable of doing that which they could never think about doing on their own: *The Spirit of truth who issues from the Father, he will be my witness. And you too will be witnesses, because you have been with me from the outset* (*Jn* 15:26b-27). John the Evangelist weighs the Master's words about the witness that the disciples were to give him in the world, in spite of the fear that some of them felt, the forgetfulness of others and the betrayal that was possible at any moment.

Throughout history, there is always a struggle taking place between darkness and light (cf. *Jn* 1:4-11), and present in this confrontation is the mystery of rejection that can affect even those closest to Christ, who asks the Father: *I am not praying for the world but for those you have given me* (*Jn* 17:9). The context is dramatic, but there is great serenity in the words of Jesus who neither keeps quiet about evil nor expresses any condemnation for it; he is worried about his people, so that they may live the times to come with knowledge and trust.

89. Like every century, our time is one of struggle between light and darkness. It is a time when relationships between nations, cultures and religions are reshaped. It is a time in which roads widen their intersections in spaces where people are forced into acceptance or rejection, even violent rejection. It is a time in which Christians are asked, with arrogant violence, about the reasons for their hope, and consecrated persons continue their story as witnesses to the Light. In the sign of charity *until the end* (cf. *Jn* 13:1), consecrated men and women have borne witness to Christ the Lord with the giving of their own lives. There are thousands

of them who, having been forced into the catacombs of persecution by totalitarian regimes and violent groups opposed to missionary work and actions to defend the poor and to assist the sick and marginalised, lived and live their consecration in prolonged and heroic suffering, often shedding their own blood, perfectly configured to the Crucified Lord. A woman missionary writes: "I am now almost in my 80s. On my last visit to Italy, my superiors were uncertain whether to let me leave. One day, during Adoration, I prayed, 'Jesus, thy will be done, but you know I still want to go'. I clearly heard in my head these words. 'Olga, do you think you will save Africa? Africa is mine. Nevertheless, I am glad you are going: Go and give your life!' From that moment on, I no longer doubted".[41]

Witness to the point of bloodshed is the distinguished seal of Christian hope: the singular glory for the Church. "I only want a place at the feet of Jesus. I want my life, my character, my actions to speak of me and say that I am following Jesus Christ. This desire is so strong in me that I consider myself privileged whenever - in my combative effort to help the needy, the poor, the persecuted Christians of Pakistan - Jesus should wish to accept the sacrifice of my life. I want to live for Christ and it is for him that I want to die. I do not feel any fear in this country".[42]

Among Christian martyrs, consecrated men and women mark an ascendant and impassioned parable: the Church is still the Church of Jesus Christ who announced persecution for his disciples. Consecrated life and the reality of martyrdom show us "where the Church is".[43]

DREAMING LIKE CHRISTIANS

90. The final message, given to us by the experience and wishes of those who participated in the *Week in Communion* that closed the Year of Consecrated Life, invites us to be glad in the hope that is so scarce and fragile in contemporary cultures and among us. We need to revive the theological reason for our hope to let it live in the Church.

---

[41] From the unpublished writings of Olga Raschietti (Montecchio Maggiore, 22nd August, 1931 Kamenge, 7th September, 2014), Missionary of Mary, killed in Burundi.

[42] Cf. C. SHAHBAZ BHATTI, *Cristiani in Pakistan. Nelle Prove la Speranza*, Marcianum Press, Venice 2008.

[43] Cf. J. RATZINGER, *Perché siamo Ancora nella Chiesa*, Rizzoli, Milan 2008, 26.

The vision of hope is generative; it joyously adheres to what the Spirit is fulfilling today. A woman religious tells us: "Now I am returning to Burundi. Though at my age I am physically weak and limited, inwardly, I think I can say that my drive and desire to be faithful to Jesus's love expressed in the mission is very much alive. The mission helps me to tell him in my weakness, 'Jesus, look, it's my gesture of love for you'".[44]

Welcoming the Spirit enables us to be creative and bold as we live our *sequela Christi* in different cultural contexts and new anthropological paradigms: "We need to nurture in ourselves a gaze of sympathy, respect and appreciation of the values of the cultures, traditions of the people we meet. Despite the complex situation and conflict in the countries of the Great Lakes, I seem to sense the presence of a Kingdom of love that is being built, growing like a mustard seed given to all. At this point in my journey, I continue to serve my African brothers, trying to live with love, simplicity and joy".[45]

We are able to lead new generations towards the future in hope by trusting in the *spring rains* (*Ho* 6:3), so that young consecrated persons can be genius and original protagonists of new change in the freedom of the Spirit.

91. Hope is the Christian dream that enlivens and illuminates life in the Church. "I love truth, which is like light, and justice, which is an essential aspect of love. I like to tell everyone things as they are, good to good and evil to evil, without calculation, with the only calculation the Gospel mentions: do good because it is good. God will take care of the consequences for the good that is done".[46] "I only have one vocation, structural I would say: even with all of the shortcomings and unworthiness possible, I am, by the Lord's grace, a witness of the Gospel: *you will be my witnesses*".[47]

---

[44] From the unpublished writings of Lucia Pulici (Desio, 8th September, 1939 Kamenge, 7th September, 2014), Missionary of Mary, killed in Burundi.

[45] From the unpublished writings of Bernadetta Boggian (Ospedaletto Euganeo, 17th March, 1935 Kamenge, 8th September, 2014) Missionary of Mary, killed in Burundi.

[46] G. LA PIRA, *Speech on 24th September, 1954* in the City Council of Florence, in A. SCIVOLETTO, Giorgio La Pira, Studium, Rome 2003, 159.

[47] G. LA PIRA, *Letter from 27th November, 1953*, in *Caro Giorgio... Caro Amintore... 25 Anni di Storia nel Carteggio La Pira-Fanfani*, edited by S. Selmi and S. Nerozzi, Polistampa, Firenze 2003, 190-195.

Giorgio La Pira continues in a letter to a consecrated female friend: "Reverend Mother, am I a bit of a dreamer? Maybe. But all of Christianity is a dream: the sweet dream of a God made into man so that man could become God! If this dream is real why would the other dreams essentially connected to this dream not be real? But it seems to me that these are not dreams, this is called Christian virtue, it is called hope".[48] The Eternal, denied by present cultures, spreads its dimension in the world also through the reasons for our hope.

HAIL, VIRGIN OF THE CENACLE

92. The Mother of Jesus and the apostles united in prayer show the nascent Church as an admirable example of concord and prayer. In the atmosphere of waiting that fills the Cenacle after the Ascension, Mary implores the gift of the Spirit. The Pentecost is also the fruit of the Blessed Virgin's incessant prayer, which is accepted by the Paraclete because it is an expression of her motherly love for the disciples. "The Holy Spirit bestows the fullness of his gifts on the Blessed Virgin and those present, working a deep transformation in them for the sake of spreading the Good News. The Mother of Christ and his disciples are granted new strength and new apostolic energy for the Church's growth".[49]

Between the Annunciation and the Pentecost the fecundity given to Mary by the Holy Spirit spreads out: "In the redemptive economy of grace, brought about through the action of the Holy Spirit, there is a unique correspondence between the moment of the Incarnation of the Word and the moment of the birth of the Church. The person who links these two moments is Mary: Mary at Nazareth and Mary in the Upper Room at Jerusalem. In both cases her discreet yet essential presence indicates the path of birth from the Holy Spirit".[50]

So it is for us: from *come and follow me* to the mandate *go and proclaim*. From the acceptance of the call to missionary fecundity. On the new paths of the Spirit.

---

[48] G. La Pira, *La Preghiera, Forza Motrice della Storia: Lettere ai Monasteri Femminili di Vita Contemplativa*, edited by V. Peri, Città Nuova, Rome 2007, 64.

[49] John Paul II, *General Audience* (May 28, 1997).

[50] John Paul II, Encyclical Letter *Redemptoris Mater* (March 25, 1987) 24; cf. Paul VI, Apostolic Exhortation *Marialis Cultus* (February 2, 1974), 28.

O Father,
as the Blessed Virgin was at prayer with the apostles in the Cenacle
you poured out on her in abundance the gifts of the Holy Spirit,
grant that the Church may persevere unanimous in prayer,
that Pentecost may be everlasting and that the holy fire
may consume every evil, and eliminate ugliness,
loneliness and burning bitterness.

Holy Father,
hear the prayers that your good Spirit places in the hearts and on the lips of those who confide in you:
deliver us from the burden of sin
that saddens and extinguishes the Spirit descended upon the Virgin given in the Cenacle
and may the Church always shine for new fruits of sanctity and grace
to bring the Good News of salvation to the world.

Vatican City, 29th June, 2016
Solemnity of Saints Peter and Paul, Apostles

João Braz Card. de Aviz
Prefect

✠ José Rodríguez Carballo, O.F.M.
Archbishop Secretary

FOR REFLECTION

93. Are our ministries, our works and our presence consonant with what the Spirit asked of our founders? Are they suitable for carrying out today, in society and the Church, those same ministries and works? Do we have the same passion for our people, are we close to them to the point of sharing in their joys and sorrows, thus truly understanding their needs and helping to respond to them? [1]

- "'Who is Jesus for the people of our time?' The world needs Christ more than ever: his salvation, his merciful love. Many people feel an empty void around and within themselves; others live in restlessness and insecurity due to uncertainty and conflict. We all need adequate answers to our questions, to our concrete questions. Only in Him, in Christ, is it possible to find true peace and the fulfilment of every human aspiration. Jesus knows the human heart better than anyone. This is why he can heal, giving life and consolation".[2]
- "Let us ask ourselves: Is our faith fruitful? Does our faith produce good works? Or is it sterile instead, and therefore more dead than alive? Do I act as a neighbour or simply pass by? Am I one of those who selects people according to my own liking? It is good to ask ourselves these questions, and to ask them often, because in the end we will be judged on the works of mercy. The Lord will say to us: Do you remember that time on the road from Jerusalem to Jericho? That man who was half dead was me. Do you remember? That hungry child was me. Do you remember? That immigrant who many wanted to drive away, that was me. That grandparent who was alone, abandoned in nursing homes, that was me. That sick man, alone in the hospital, who no one visited, that was me".[3]

---

[1] Cf. Francis, Apostolic Letter *To all Consecrated People on the Occasion of the Year of Consecrated Life* (21st November, 2014), I, 2.

[2] Francis, *Angelus* (19th June, 2016).

[3] Francis, *Angelus* (10th July, 2016).

- "The gift Jesus offers is the fullness of life for a hungering mankind. Jesus satiates not only material hunger, but the most profound one, the hunger for the meaning of life, the hunger for God. Before the suffering, loneliness, poverty and difficulties of so many people, what can we ourselves do? Complaining doesn't resolve anything, but we can offer the little that we have, like the lad in the Gospel [...] Who among us doesn't have 'five loaves and two fish' of his own? We all have them! If we are willing to place them in the Lord's hands, they will be enough to bring about a little more love, peace, justice and especially joy in the world".[4]

- "What does it mean for our communities and for each one of us to belong to a Church which is catholic and apostolic? First of all, it means *taking the salvation of all mankind to heart*, not feeling indifferent or alien in facing the fate of so many of our brothers and sisters, but open and sympathetic toward them. It means, moreover, *having a sense of the fullness, the completeness, the harmony* of the Christian life, always rejecting partisan, unilateral positions, which close us within ourselves. [...] And here I would like to recall the heroic life of so very many missionaries, men and women who left their homeland in order to go to proclaim the Gospel in other countries, on other continents. A Brazilian Cardinal who works quite often in Amazonia, was telling me that when he goes to a place, to a village or a town in Amazonia, he always goes to the cemetery where he sees the tombs of these missionaries, priests, brothers, sisters who went to preach the Gospel: apostles. And he thinks: all of them could be canonised now, they left all in order to proclaim Jesus Christ".[5]

---

[4] FRANCIS, *Angelus* (26th July, 2015).

[5] FRANCIS, *General Audience* (17th September, 2014).

- "Evangelising the poor: this is Jesus's mission. According to what he says, this is also the mission of the Church, and of every person baptised in the Church. Being a Christian is the same thing as being a missionary. Proclaiming the Gospel with one's word, and even before, with one's life, is the primary aim of the Christian community and of each of its members. [...] Jesus addresses the Good News to all, excluding no one, indeed favouring those who are distant, suffering sick, cast out by society. Let us ask ourselves: what does it mean to evangelise the poor? It means first of all drawing close to them, it means having the joy of serving them, of freeing them from their oppression, and all of this in the name of and with the Spirit of Christ, because he is the Gospel of God, he is the Mercy of God, he is the liberation of God, he is the One who became poor so as to enrich us with his poverty".[6]

[6] Francis, *Angelus* (24th January, 2016).